The Outcast

W. Winwood Reade

The Outcast

Contact:
IndoEuropeanPublishing@gmail.com

The present edition is a reproduction of 1933 publication of this work, produced in the current edition with completely new, easy to read format by Indo-European Publishing.

For an authentic reading experience, the Spelling, punctuation, and capitalization have been retained from the original text.

Cover Design by Indo-European Design Team

ISBN: 978-1-60444-609-8

IndoEuropean
Publishing.com
Los Angeles, CA, USA

Introduction

MANY readers of The Martyrdom of Man must have speculated upon the character and the fate of the other books written by the same hand. It seems on the face of it incredible that a work which, on its first appearance in 1872, won its way to popular favor in spite of total neglect or unbridled condemnation by the newspapers and reviews, and in spite of its slashing onslaughts upon accepted opinions, should stand quite alone. No favorable review of this disturbing volume appeared until 1906, yet edition after edition bore witness to a steady demand. Even upon the post-war generation, to whom the successes of the Victorian age mean less than nothing, Winwood Reade's vision of the world has cast its spell. Within ten years fully one hundred thousand copies have passed into circulation. No shadow of mortality has yet fallen upon its pages. Is there nothing else among his writings that yet lives?

If this question had to be answered without qualification in the negative, an adequate explanation might be given on two grounds. Winwood Reade died young, at the age of thirty-six — an age when, in the comparatively slow-maturing period during which he lived, achievement might be expected to have only begun. Moreover, his earlier writings were written in fiction form, to which his powers were not well adapted. In choosing the vehicle of fiction Winwood

Reade was probably inspired by the example of his famous uncle, Charles Reade, who was fresh risen to fame at the time when Winwood was at Oxford. Before he was twenty-one Winwood published a short novel, 'Charlotte and Myra,' following this a year later with a three-decker 'Liberty Hall, Oxon,' in which the lives of undergraduates were portrayed. Both were failures, and the disappointment over these early ventures may have had something to do with their author's decision, in 1862, to visit Africa as an explorer. It was in Africa, during a series of adventurous journeys, followed by experiences as 'The Times' correspondent during the Ashanti War, that he gathered much of the material woven later into 'The Martyrdom of Man.' During 1865 another novel appeared — 'See-Saw,' a story dealing with Roman Catholicism in Italy and Protestantism in England — but it was no more fortunate than its predecessors. In his 'African Sketch Book' Reade confessed that "my books are literary insects, doomed to a trifling and ephemeral existence, to buzz and hum for a season — and to die."

The books in which he recorded his African adventures were somewhat more fortunate, though they failed to bring him his due recognition as an intrepid explorer. According to Mr. F. Legge, "the cause which chiefly contributed to the public neglect of his results was the extraordinary form in which he thought fit to publish them. They did not appear at all until three years after his return to England, and then only in the form of a journal kept while in the bush for the perusal of a lady whom he addresses as 'Dear Margaret,' and for whom he seems to have had a deep and tender affection." Further, although this work, the 'African Sketch Book,' contained much solid information on anthropological matters and several good maps, it "was stuffed with tales of savage life which are avowedly, like the illustrations with which it abounds, drawn from the imagination merely."

Only in 'The Martyrdom of Man,' in an earlier work 'The Veil of Isis' (1861) recounting the history of the Druids, and in 'The Story of the Ashanti Campaign,' which amplifies his contributions to The Times, does Winwood Reade make a definite departure from the fictional model at which he first tried his hand. It is significant, therefore, that in his last book, 'The Outcast,' he returns to this model and uses it as a vehicle for the expression of his deepest thoughts on the problems of life — or, rather, the problem of life.

'The Outcast' was written during his last illness. His strength had been undermined during his earlier journeys in Africa, and the dysentery and fever contracted in the Ashanti campaign broke down his last defenses. Death was near, and in the nearness of death he penned his brief and eloquent confession of faith. It was published in 1875 — the year of his, death — and within that year it had passed into a third edition.

Since then 'The Outcast' has not, until now, been reprinted. But it has not been forgotten. Copies have been treasured by their possessors and passed to trusted and discerning friends. The passage of time has proved that although the book cannot rival 'The Martyrdom of Man' in magnitude or brilliance, and although the treatment recalls the conventions of an age that seems almost archaic, it has the touch of greatness and the universal appeal that defy time and change. Each generation as it emerges to the stage of conscious reflection confronts anew the ancient puzzle of the existence of evil. Each of us must, in our own way, settle our account with a universe which involves the martyrdom of man. Here, through the medium of a story which is really a philosophical essay, Winwood Reade discusses more than one solution, from the bankrupt evasion of suicide to the illusory prospect of compensation in another world where the errors of omniscience shall be made good. His own solution is finally offered — a solution based on the frank acceptance of facts of life, sinister and cheerful alike, and culminates in the faith that man may, by the exercise of reason and goodwill, become the master of a happier destiny. He finds joy and fulfillment in a religion of service: "To labor and love without hope of requital or reward, what religion could be more pure and more sublime?"

A few days after Winwood Reade's death, Charles Reade wrote that he had died "heir to considerable estates which he did not live long enough to inherit, and gifted with genius which he had no time to mature." While this is a just estimate, we may console ourselves with the though that during his short span Winwood Reade lived intensely, thought deeply, and gave expression to his zeal for intellectual honesty and his fervor for human betterment in two volumes which still illumine the mind and touch the heart.

Letter I

MY DEAR FRANK, — I welcome you back to your native land, and take it for granted that you and Ellen are tired enough of travelling. Life in a strange country is always artificial — it seems to me like being at a play — and constant change becomes monotonous after a time. I hear from Ellen that she intends to stop in London a week before joining you at home; and I shall reserve till then my latest budget of news about the tenants, and the harvest, and the pets, and the penny readings, &c. just now I can think of little else but the tragedy at Dr. Scott's, some account of which no doubt you have seen in the papers. But I will tell you the whole story.

Arthur Elliott was the only son of a wealthy landed proprietor, one of my nearest neighbors, and a brother magistrate. Arthur had a most amiable nature, and was tenderly loved, not only by his parents, but by all who knew him intimately. His attainments were remarkable, as I can testify; for we read much together. He was an excellent classical scholar, but his favorite study was that of metaphysics, from which he was led to the study of natural science. Religion was the poetry and passion of his life; and, though of a different belief, it afforded me pleasure to hear him discourse on the grandeur and benevolence of God. Sometimes when we were together in a deep green wood on a sultry summer afternoon; or sometimes walking at night beneath the glorious starlit sky; or sometimes when reading the dialogues of Plato, some divine thought rose from the book like an immortal spirit from the grave,

4

and passed into his soul; then the tears would stream from his eyes, and falling on his knees he would utter praises or prayers in words of surpassing eloquence, and with a voice of the sweetest melody. And often — how well I remember it now — often at such times his gestures grew wild and almost furious, his utterance was choked, and a strange bubbling sound came from his mouth. Dr. Scott, who was present on one of these occasions, watched him I thought, with an air of anxiety; and I heard that he advised the Elliotts to take away their son from his books and send him abroad with a travelling tutor. But Arthur disliked the idea of leaving home, and his parents did not urge him to go, believing that the danger was imaginary. So he remained, and things went on as before.

One day he came to me in trouble. He had been reading the great work of Malthus — the 'Essay on Population' — and said that it made him doubt the goodness of God. I replied with the usual common-place remarks; he listened to me attentively, then sighed, shook his head, and went away. A little while afterwards he read 'The Origin of Species,' which had just come out, and which proves that the Law of Population is the chief agent by which Evolution has been produced. From that time he began to show symptoms of insanity — which disease, it is thought, he inherited from one of his progenitors. He dressed always in black, and said that he was in mourning for mankind. The works of Malthus and Darwin, bound in somber covers, were placed on a table in his room; the first was lettered outside 'The Book of Doubt,' and the second 'The Book of Despair.' He took long solitary walks in the most secluded parts of the estate, and was sometimes seen gesticulating to the heavens, sometimes seated by the wayside plucking grass and casting it from him with a strange, tremulous movement of the hands. It was in vain that his good parents and the rector attempted to soothe his troubled mind with the hopes and consolations of a future life. He said that a wrong was always a wrong, and that no reward could atone for unmerited punishment. It was then I thought it right to express my own opinions on the subject of theology. But, though Arthur could cease to love and revere, he could not cease to believe. I have often observed that men of powerful intellect, especially those of the poetic constitution, find it almost impossible to shake off the faith which has been taught them in their childhood. In Arthur's case the boldest spirit of inquiry and a remorseless power of induction were allied to a rigid habit of belief. If he could have closed his eyes, in common with so many inquirers, to the barbarous element in nature, or simply dismissed it from his mind after a brief period of discomfort, he might have continued to believe in the God of his imagination and preserved his happiness. If, on the other hand, unable to escape from positive fact, he could have given up, or doubted ever so little, the dogma of a Personal Creator, he would, I believe, have finally found repose. As it was, he fell into a most deplorable condition. His God had never been an abstraction, but a Father and a Friend; and now, by ever brooding on the subject, by ever directing his thoughts towards this Imaginary Person, he actually felt its presence, as the hermit in the desert after months of contemplation, as the cenobite in the solitary cell. With him, however, it was not love and devotion, it was anger and hatred, which kindled the dangerous fire in the brain, inspired the vision, and forced him to commune with the shadow of his mind.

He spent much of his time with me, and at last I wearied of his complaints. I told him that it was useless to repine against the Inexorable; that after all there was more good than evil in the world if we went the right way to find it; and that if he sympathized so much with the miseries of men he should try to mitigate them, instead of pouring forth idle lamentations. He looked at me sadly, and embraced me, resting his head upon my shoulder; he never spoke of his troubles again, and I often repented of my harshness. But not long afterwards we all thought that he was saved. He became betrothed to a lovely and charming girl, Miss Lilian Moore, who was visiting at the rectory. She seemed to possess some tranquillizing power; her eyes, were calm and deep, and goodness was written in every feature of her face. She saw that Arthur required occupation, and asked him to compose some stories to amuse her. He complied, and wrote a number of tales, in which the trees, and flowers, and rocks, and animals were his characters and heroes. These stories were fanciful, quaint, and humorous; and several being published in the magazines, attracted notice from the press. Arthur received more than one flattering offer from London publishing firms, and began to show himself ambitious of literary fame. He had now quite recovered his health and happiness; he saw Lilian every day; but ah, Frank, how shall I tell you, the dear girl caught an infectious fever from nursing a sick child in the village, and died. Arthur went to the funeral, but sat a little way off on the tombstone plucking the grass and casting it from him with the strange movement of the hands I mentioned before. As the service was ended the clock struck twelve. He got up and said, "The wedding will be late!" and approached the grave which had just been filled up. Then he flung himself upon it with fearful shrieks and curses against the supposed Author of the world. When people attempted to lead him away he dashed them to the ground with superhuman strength. Yet even in this fearful attack of mania he seemed to recognize his father, and only shrank back from the aged hands carousingly placed upon his arm. He was taken to Dr. Scott's private asylum, which was but a little way from the church, and in a few days ceased to be violent, asked for his papers and books, and, having obtained them studied from morning to night. He appeared perfectly quiet and contented; but every night, when the church clock struck twelve, he opened the window of his room, which was on the ground floor, murmured the name of Lilian, folded his arms upon his breast, as if he had embraced her, and kissed the air. Then, with the connivance of his servant, he sprang out of the window and walked to the churchyard, followed by the man, who at least never let him go out of his sight. All the while he conversed (as if with Lilian) in the most animated manner, and, having reached the grave, made movements with his hands as if covering her up; after which he said "Good-night" in a cheerful voice and returned. These promenades were, of course, discovered in time. Arthur was carefully watched, the servant was dismissed, the windows were barred. Nothing else could have been done, yet there is too much reason to fear that this restraint proved injurious. When the hour of midnight drew near he became uneasy and restless; and when prevented from going to the window be fell into a state of dejection.

He no longer slept well, and was often troubled with visions and dreams. One morning, when he awoke, he sat up in bed, and laughed till the tears ran out of his eyes. He sent for the doctor, and told him he had "found it all out," and, when asked to explain what he meant, replied that it was an original idea — a most important discovery — and that he should send it to a magazine. "If I told you what it was," he continued, "you would keep me here all my life, and pass off my idea on a deluded public as your own." The doctor, to humor him, replied that he was incapable of such malpractice. "Ah, well!" replied Arthur, "at ordinary times, and in ordinary cases, no doubt you are an honest man; but here the temptation would be too strong. Still, I don't mind telling you my title. It's 'A New Thing under the Moon.'" He then burst out laughing again, and rubbed his hands together with glee. In the afternoon he became violent, said he should "throw up his part," and tried to spring out of the window, dashing himself against the bars. He was placed in a padded room. The next day he was quiet as usual, and asked for paper and ink; but as the doctor wished to get him to sleep, of which he stood in much need, this request was refused. At first he seemed angry, then shrugged his shoulders and smiled. It was afterwards found that he had a note-book and pencil in his pocket. At ten o'clock p.m. he appeared drowsy, but said that he could not sleep with people in the room; and Dr. Scott told the attendants to go outside, but to look in from time to time. In an hour or so he seemed to fall into a sleep, which was probably assumed, and the vigilance of the watchers was relaxed. But in the grey hour of the dawn they heard a struggle in the room and a choked kind of cry. They pushed the door, but it had been secured from within by a small piece of wood wedged in underneath. They forced it open at last, and the body of the unfortunate young man was found hanging from the window bar. Life was extinct. On the table was a note-book in which he had been writing. Dr. Scott has just sent it over, and advises me to read it; so in my next letter I may give you an account of its contents. Such, dear son-in-law, is the sad history of Arthur Elliott.

Letter II

MY DEAR FRANK, — I enclose you a copy of Elliott's last production, written in a state of insanity, just before he committed suicide. It will reach you, I hope, before. Ellen's return, as I suppose you would not wish her to see it. You make it a rule, I know, not to discuss theology with women, and I am much of your opinion. When Ellen was a girl I carefully attended to the culture of her mind, and encouraged her to read works of philosophy and science. But, though I saw that she possessed a vigorous intellect, I did not dare to carry her beyond the limits of Theism. I feared that for her my faith would be but a system of cold and comfortless philosophy, and that if at some future time, in adversity or suffering, a religion became necessary to her, she would run no slight risk of falling into Superstition. I saved her from that danger by teaching her to believe in a God, compared with whom the God of the Bible is a very indifferent character. But I need not say that my God, though a nobler conception, is just as much a creature of fiction as the other. They are both made by human heads, as idols are made by human hands; only, while the people of the churches and the chapels worship an idol of brass, I gave my daughter an idol of gold. I formed her a God of the purest and noblest ideas, and she still believes it to be real. Of course, some day or other she may discover the deception; and were she to read the enclosed manuscript, she would, I think, cease to believe in the Divine benevolence, and next would begin to suspect that the Being called God is as much a fabulous creature as Jupiter, Mars, or Apollo. And then comes the great question, "Would she be able to accept our religion, which demands such an utter abnegation of self? Would she even understand it?" I fear that she would lapse into that state of skepticism and indifference which, in a woman at least, is more odious and harmful than superstition.

I therefore advise you not to show her this manuscript. But read it yourself without delay, for you will be able to enjoy it. It will not make you tremble in your shoes. You have climbed above theology, as the Alpine mountaineer above the clouds.

A New Thing Under The Moon

The habit of reading in bed is delightful, but the books used for that purpose should be carefully selected. It was most imprudent of me to read, and at Dr. Scott's of all places in the world, the 'Confessions of an Opium-Eater' just after three chapters of Butler's Analogy. I might have known that it would give me mental indigestion. Needless to say that I had a dream, and such a dream! or rather such a series of dreams! Yet, though I spent a bad night, it is some consolation to reflect it was so ordained for the good of mankind. I am willing indeed to admit that the system of Cosmogony set forth in my dream may possibly not be true, and I shall not claim for it the name of Revelation as other dreamers have done; I merely assert that my theory of Cause and Creation is the best that has ever been propounded. It explains all the facts of history and nature, is in harmony with science, and is supported by analogy. Above all, it is quite original; nothing like it has ever been imagined before; and, though Solomon wisely observes that there is no new thing under the Sun, there may be a new thing under the Moon; and dreams are exceptions to every rule. However, my readers shall judge for themselves

I dreamt, first of all, I was standing, as it seemed to me, in Space, and I had a curious kind of impression that the Infinite was not too large, but just the right size for a person of my dimensions. I observed something in the distance of a dark and shadowy appearance, in form like a promontory, of which I could plainly perceive the extremity or point, but not the base and middle parts, although, as the point was exactly opposite my range of vision, and was turned away from me, it was clear that the bulk of the promontory must be situated between me and the extremity in question. This puzzled me much, and after staring some time I closed my left eye in order to see more distinctly. Then up shot a huge wall to the left of my right and still open eye. If you look at your nose with both eyes open, and then look at it with one eye shut, you will understand what I mean. I had, in fact, been surveying the tip of my own nose, which was distant many thousand miles from the middle of my face. I glanced at my shoulders, but they extended indefinitely into space; I could not see either of my hands, they were too far off; and when I lifted one up it seemed like a huge flesh-colored mountain sailing towards me through the air, and threatening to crush me if I did not pull it back. Then I thought what a dreadful thing it was to have such a nose, and a body which could be measured only by means of a trigonometrical survey. A cold perspiration broke out on my forehead, and I calculated that each drop was about the size of the Atlantic Ocean. This woke me with a start. I sat up in bed, felt my nose, and then, cursing all opium-eaters, lay down and fell asleep again.

I next dreamt that I was seated in an amphitheater or circus, in the midst of a large audience. I was conscious that I had the same body as before, and that all the persons present were equally enormous; yet I could see the ends of my shoulders, and my nose did not seem to be long; the reason of which I suppose to be this — that in my previous dream I was in a transitional state; my body had become that of the Demigods, whose kingdom I had entered, while my eyesight remained in the human condition. But now my vision had also been enlarged, and I soon found that it possessed extraordinary powers.

The arena of the circus must have been many millions of miles in extent, and was a bottomless pit of pure ether, traversed by a bright shining ball, round which sailed a number of dark little beads attending its course. Now I fancied I had seen them somewhere before. I looked at them again more attentively, — there could be no doubt at all about the matter, — it was the Solar System.

My mind was still that of a mortal; so, instead of looking down on our little universe with the calm curiosity of a superior being, I had the injured feeling of an inhabitant, and rose to go, saying, "It is only an ornery after all."

However, I observed that the eyes of the spectators were all turned in the direction of the Earth; so I looked at it too; and then, oh, wonder of wonders what did I behold!

I could see the whole globe, and everything upon it, even worlds of animalcule too minute to be distinguished with the best microscopes; even the waves of light, invisible to mortals, which break upon the surface of the Earth like the waves of the sea upon the shore. I could see every man woman, and child, and study their actions without effort or confusion. I could view, at the same time, numberless dramas of domestic life which were being performed within the dramas of the nations; while these were only parts of the great drama of the Earth. It is, of course, difficult to explain how so many different objects could be at the same time gathered by the eye, transmitted to the brain, and assimilated by the intellect. It would be difficult to explain to a maggot how the eye of a man can take in a landscape at a glance. Yet these powers of vision will not seem excessive when the size of the eye is taken into consideration. I should say that the pupil of a demigod's eye is about double the sun's diameter, and no doubt, if dissected, would be found to contain lenses of extraordinary structure. But I have merely to record facts and am not called upon to offer explanations.

The pleasure I derived at first from looking at the Earth was soon marred by the fearful tragedies which I saw everywhere enacted. It was nearly all blood and tears; and, unable to gaze any longer on the torture of my kind, I rose to leave the theater. At the same time one of the audience went out, followed by a titter from the crowd, and I recognized in him the likeness of an historical personage; or, rather, the historical personage was a likeness of him. Then I understood that this earth-life of ours is only a satirical play, that our great men are caricatures of famous demigods, their vicissitudes and actions, ingenious lampoons. And is this all? thought I to myself. Are we with our proud aspirations only as puppets in a show? Are love, ambition, and religious sentiment — the tremulous passion, the desire of fame, the divine yearnings of the soul — are these but as the jerkings of a wire cunningly contrived? Are the terrible combats of life as gladiator- games to make the demigods a holiday? Ah, then it is sad! and yet do not men as it is often martyr their lives to make a noise in the world and gain the plaudits of a human audience? And should not we who aspire to greatness rejoice that we play before the Immortals, and may hope to achieve celestial fame? Thus I tried to console my suffering heart; but alas! it was in vain. I had a hope — one last hope — and now it was destroyed. For I saw that the dead cannot be united, since we are but as shadows that vanish away. All is lost, all is done; farewell for ever, Lilian: farewell, my only love, for evermore.

I fled into Space. But I found that the senses of hearing and smell were endowed with powers not less marvelous than those of the sight. Though now far away, I could smell the Earth, which gave forth a carrion stench not only from its body but its soul. Each vice had its horrible odor. It is true that each virtue had its fragrance as well, and sometimes, though rarely, a breath of perfume floated through the air. And now strange sounds arose. I heard the humming of the Earth as it spun, and the roaring of the fire in its innermost depths. I heard the whispers of conscience and the chidings of remorse, the sighs of unrequited love, the cries of many agonies. At the same time I heard the audience hooting and shouting, Off! off! Shame! Apologize! Where is the Lord Chamberlain? But in the midst of this turmoil the cries of anguish were hushed, a sweet balmy smell was diffused through space, the voices of the earth rose in a strain of enchanting melody, and thunders of applause seemed to indicate that the drama was concluded. Then I woke up and found my cheeks all wet with tears which I had shed.

My servant, who is very attentive — perhaps a little over- attentive — has taken my lamp away, but there is a splendid moon, and I am writing near the window by its light. I do not understand why, the day after my dream, they put me into this room, which is not so large as my own, and furnished in very bad taste, the walls being stuffed like a first-class carriage on a railway. Where are my books? What mean those sentinel footsteps outside, the door stealthily opened, and the cold grey eyes which search into my soul? Ha! ha! ha! Look at those little black imps dancing in the moonlight on the floor! Patter, patter, patter! pit-a-pat, pit-a- pat! Ah! Lilian, my dear, you should not come out at night in that thin white shroud, and it's no use your coming here any more. The windows are barred, and I can't take you home to the quiet churchyard and put you to bed in your cozy little grave. We can meet no more by the light of the moon. Besides, it is but a play; we should only be amusing the people up there. Oh! cruel Author, why did you kill her? — in the first act, too; very inartistic. At least I don't know. As this life is a penny-gaff sort of performance, it was more effective to do it when she was young, for if she was old and ugly no one would care. But who could see her die then with the beauty of girlhood still blushing upon her, and her death caught nursing the poor sick child; who could see her die then without being smitten to the heart? It must have brought down the house. Weep, ye gods, weep your oceanic tears, and wait your sighs in gentle gales to mourn poor Lilian. And her lover lying on the grave, digging at the ground with his nails and teeth, seized, bound hand and foot, and then brought here. Oh, no doubt it was a fine stroke of art — most charmingly devised. Well, it's a hard world, and we cannot all be kings and queens; to one is the part of the villain — he is hissed; to another the maiden in distress; and poor Mad Tom must be played too.

I kept myself awake, for I feared another dream; but the odors of the earth lingered in my nostrils, and its horrible cries still sounded in my ears. After all, I thought it was best to sleep if I could. Luckily, the last number of the 'Quarterly Review' happened to be in the room, and I knew that Dr. Scott recommends this publication in cases of sleeplessness and nervous excitement. The article I selected was a perfect soporific — an essay on the Darwinian Theory, and before I had finished the preamble it had sent me to sleep. But on that fatal night even the 'Quarterly Review' could not prevent me from dreaming; and, in fact, I dreamt of a review, for my third dream took me to a Demigod club where I found the following critique in a periodical lying on the table. I wrote it from memory as soon as I awoke.

The Review

The custom of creating worlds, and of peopling them with animated beings who reflect the vices or follies of the day, or offer an example of ideal virtues and moral excellence, has of late become popular in art; and, though it may be a fashion which, like others of its kind, will soon pass away, it is in the meantime for us, who are critics and censors, to pass judgment on all such works as succeed in obtaining the attention of the public. The anonymous drama which has just been performed is said to be a first attempt; and this we should have inferred from internal evidence. For, though the work is by no means deficient in power, and contains some original ideas, there is a want of symmetry in form and of finish in detail, a prodigal waste of raw material, a roughness of style and execution which bear the stamp of inexperience. However, as will be shown, it is chiefly on moral grounds that we think this production ought to be condemned.

The work is simple in conception and modest in design. We have not here, as in some ambitious compositions, a number of inhabited worlds contributing each its part to the story. One system only is placed upon the stage, and the action is confined to one planet of that system.

At first the world was presented to our view as a fiery cloud. It became compressed to a Sun, which advanced through Space, rotating on its axis, and cast off certain pieces from itself like tyres from a wheel. These cooled into planetary bodies, and one of them, called by its inhabitants 'The Earth,' was the scene of the drama which we shall now endeavor to describe. We observed with unmixed pleasure the gradual growth of the planet from a cinder enveloped in cloud to a globe covered with water; the sun-rays causing the origin of life; the floating animalcules and one-celled plants; the rise of the land from the deep, and its naked skin being clothed with a green mantle of palm and fern vegetation. Monstrous reptiles and ungainly quadrupeds inhabited the primeval marshes of the earth; and at night the croaking of enormous frogs rose like thunder in the air. But as time flowed on the face of the earth assumed a more gentle and benignant expression; flowers blossomed in the forest, and the voices of singing birds were heard;

15

the quadrupeds became less gigantic in size, but more graceful and varied in their forms; and finally Men appeared upon the scene, roaming in herds through the forest, clambering the trees, jabbering semi-articulate sounds. But, as language formed upon their lips, the erect posture was assumed, the fore-foot was used as a hand, weapons were invented, fire was discovered, caverns in the rock, burrows in the ground, and platforms on the trees were exchanged for huts surrounded by gardens. Wild animals were tamed, the seed-bearing grasses were cultured into grain, canoes glided on the waters, commerce became the rival of war, which, once incessant, was now occasional. The tribes were united into nations, the nations into empires, great cities flourished on the banks of rivers and by harbors on the sea-shore; classes were divided, the arts and sciences arose. At first these were kept as state secrets, and often perished with the state. At first wealth, culture, and power belonged exclusively to the dominant caste, while the masses labored in subjection. But by means of useful inventions knowledge was widely diffused, and the passion for liberty entered the bosom of the people. One nation after another shook itself free from the tyranny of kings and the tyranny of priests. When class restrictions were removed all could hope by honest labor to better their condition, and all striving for their own ends assisted the onward movement of the world. At a later period the social equality of men extinguished personal ambition, and the Welfare of the Race was the aim of those who labored for distinction. Fame could be obtained only by adding something to the knowledge or the happiness of men. Finally war ceased; the malignant forces of Nature were subdued, vice and disease were eradicated, the earth became a pleasure garden, and men learnt to bear without repining a painless death in extreme old age.

We suppose that the moral purpose of this drama is to teach the doctrine of Improvement, and to illustrate that tendency to Progress which pervades the universe. The evolution of mind from matter, by means of natural law, shows the innate power of that tendency or force, and the efforts by which Man achieves his own comparative perfection are no doubt intended as a protest against that habit of quiescence and content which is perhaps the natural failing of Immortals. We think that the satire on theology is wholesome and just. Nothing could be more ludicrous than to see these ephemeral beings, these creatures of a moment, building little houses in honor of the First Cause and glibly explaining mysteries which we do not profess to understand. This may serve as a warning to certain presumptuous philosophers who fabricate theories respecting the Supreme; for how can we know that we are not in the same relative position to beings of a higher race as those pygmies we create to ourselves? At least it is certain that our intellects, great as they are, or great as we think them to be, are unable to explain primary phenomena or to solve the problems of Cause, Existence, and Futurity. So far then we go with our author; and in numberless ways he has justly derided the follies of our race. We can afford to forgive him for creating human reviewers to parody our profession, the more so as coarse caricature fails of its effect; but we must object to the introduction of personal portraits; it was settled long ago as a dogma in art that mere copies should have no place in a creation. This, however, is not a defect on which we shall dwell, for, though in itself serious enough, it is light and trivial when compared with the faults it is now our duty to expose.

In the first place, it is most degrading that these men who are made in our image, who in their exterior form and mental faculties partly resemble ourselves, should be suffered to retain both in body and mind so much of the lower animals. The Creator may, perhaps, reply that he laid down the law of gradual transition, and that all traces of the beast in man could not be expelled except by departing from the law. But since he transformed, by gradual transition, the muzzle or snout to the lips of beauty radiant with smiles, the hairy paw to the skilful and delicate hand, he might surely have found some way to obliterate by change the instincts and actions of which we complain. No one can deny that he is ingenious enough when he chooses; the shark's jaw and the serpent's fang are models of dexterous contrivance, though we do not envy him these inventions. In any case, the difficulty is one of his own making, and if he could have devised no other plan he should have modified his law of evolution. It might have been less philosophical, but it would have been more decent; and we must own that we prefer an error in art to an outrage on decorum.

Secondly, the development of matter to mind, of quadruped to man, of savage to civilized nations, is laudable enough as an idea; but how has it been carried out? As regards the first stage of the progress we have only to praise and admire; but how has progress been produced in the animated world? We are almost ashamed to explain a law which, in its recklessness of life and prodigality of pain, almost amounts to a crime. In cold forethought the Creator so disposed the forces of nature that more animated beings were born than could possibly obtain subsistence on the earth. This caused a struggle for existence, a desperate and universal war; the best and improved animals were alone able to survive, and so in time Evolution was produced. We shall not deny that there is a kind of perverted ingenuity in the composition of this law; but the waste of life is not less clumsy than it is cruel. By means of this same struggle for existence, man was raised from the bestial state and his early discoveries were made. Afterwards, ambition of fame, and later still more noble motives came into force, but that was towards the conclusion of the drama. At first, every step in the human progress was won by conflict, and every invention resulted from calamity. The most odious vices and crimes were at one time useful to humanity, while war, tyranny, and superstition assisted the development of man.

Evil unhappily exists, and we do not condemn its employment in art. We are not in favor of those impossible dramas in which only the virtues are displayed. But we do condemn this confusion of evil and good, and maintain that nothing can be more immoral than to make crime the assistant of progress and vice the seed of which virtue is the fruit.

Again, Death is a useful and perhaps indispensable appliance in works of this kind, but so potent a means of exciting sympathy should be employed with moderation. Now what do we find here?

The law of evolution is the law of death. Massacre is incessant; flowers, animals, and men die at every moment; the earth is a vast slaughter-house, and the ocean reddened with blood. Nor, incredible as it may seem, is that the worst. With a talent for torture which rouses our wonder only next to our disgust, the Creator has smitten the animated world, even to the insects, with numerous painful and lingering diseases, while the intellect is also afflicted with maladies peculiar to itself. The affections which at first would appear to afford some meager consolation in the martyrdom of man are themselves too often the cause of mental pain and incurable despair. What can be said for such a world? What kind of defence or excuse can there be for its Creator? It is true that he made men himself, but that does not justify his cruelty. The Supreme has endowed us with the power of producing and destroying animated forms, but so terrible a gift should not be abused. We should never forget that though these little creatures live only for a moment, they are yet sentient beings, and their torments while they last are real and intense. Who could view that melancholy Earth and those writhing masses of humanity, who could hear those agonizing cries without a shudder of pain and a glow of honest indignation against the Author of such woes and wrongs? Many of the audience withdrew, while others hooted the Creator, and at one time we thought his planet would be damned. But, all's well that ends well is the easy maxim of a pleasure-seeking world, and the public, fickle and easily impressed, applauded the virtuous finale and forgot the horrors that had gone before. We were unable to do so, and declare that it seemed to us a most cruel and immoral exhibition. That is what we have to say. We know nothing of the author, but if we should meet him at a future time shall be happy to hear what he can say to exonerate himself. We do not wish to be too hard upon a young beginner whose talents cannot be disputed, and we trust that this critique, which is not unkindly meant in spite of its severity, will induce him to reform. When next he produces a world let it be one which we can take our wives and daughters to see, which will excite in the audience none but the nobler sentiments, and which also, we must add, will give us a more favorable impression of the personal character of its Creator.

Letter III

So, Ellen, you have been into Bluebeard's chamber; you have read the manuscript; and these ravings of a lunatic have made you doubt the existence of a Personal God. You suspect that I doubt it too. My dear, you are wrong; I disbelieve it. There is no doubt in my mind about the matter.

Oh, Daughter of Eve, an apple from the Tree of Knowledge was hidden in a drawer; then came the serpent Curiosity; and now, having eaten, you are banished from the Eden of belief. You wish me to tell you the whole truth, or what I believe to be the truth. Well, it can do you no harm in the present condition of your mind and may do you good — though as to that I am not very sanguine. But I will not merely expound my religious opinions; I will describe their birth and growth in my mind. I will tell you the story of my life.

Ah! the story of my life. ... Apart from all matters of religion it will deeply, too deeply, interest you. I fear, my darling, it will give you much pain; yet it is right that you should hear it; and you will be inclined more than ever, I believe, to pity and succor the unfortunate when you learn in what misery your childhood was passed.

You tell me that sometimes when you approach anything that is dead, a strange and horrible scene rises like a picture to your mind. You see a bare and squalid room — the walls blackened with dirt, the broken window-panes stuffed with rags. On the floor a woman with long yellow hair; beside her a man on his knees dressed in a ragged black coat; behind him some men and women of coarse and evil countenance, yet grave and sad, whispering together.

You shall now learn what was this scene which your memory has faithfully though fitfully retained. You shall learn how your father was an outcast, reduced to the extremity of sorrow, to the brink of despair; how his misfortunes resembled, but exceeded, those of the unhappy Elliott, and how narrowly he escaped a similar fate.

20

Letter IV

IN the last century an East India nabob named Mordaunt returned to England with an immense fortune, said to have been obtained in no very creditable manner from the treasury of a Rajah in Bengal at whose court he was Resident. My father, his only son, inherited several landed estates and a large sum of money in the funds. He was sent to Eton and Christchurch, at which latter place of education he chiefly distinguished himself as an athlete; he also rode hard across country, was a noted skittle-player, and had gained much academic fame by successfully bruising with bargees. But all this came to an end before he left the university, for he went to hear a noted field-preacher, intending to create a disturbance, and was converted on the spot. He gave up his old habits and companions, read hard for his degree, went into orders, and took the living of Harborne-in-the-Moors, which was in his own presentation. Such is the account of his youth, which I received from the excellent Bishop of T——, who was his contemporary. There was nothing in my father's appearance to show that he had ever been inclined to dissipation, or even to innocent pleasure. His features were inexpressibly severe; his eyes were cold and hard, and overhung with thick, bushy eyebrows; his lips were thin and Closely compressed. His strength was great, as I, when a boy, knew to my cost; and even his hands had a stern aspect, being broad and powerful, the spaces between the knuckles covered with long, black hairs. He did not send me to school, but taught me Greek, Latin, mathematics, and divinity himself; and seldom, I believe, has any apprentice been more harshly treated by his master. However, I ought to remind you that I was born in a flogging, cudgelling age, and that humanity to schoolboys is a virtue of recent growth. Moreover, my father was not indulgent to himself, and no paid tutor, however conscientious, would have toiled as he did with me. His day's work was almost incredible. He rose at daybreak, and read Hebrew and theology till breakfast: if it was winter, he laid and lighted his own fire. The forenoon and afternoon he devoted to me, except at two intervals which I spent in amusement, he in attending to the duties of his parish. He allowed me to pass the evenings with my mother while he corrected my exercises, and studied the lessons of the next day in Homer, Aristotle, Virgil, or Tacitus, comparing the various readings and referring to the German commentators and critics as if he were preparing an exhaustive treatise on the subject. His religion was of the lowest Calvinistic type, but at least it was sincere. He allowed himself no pleasures of any kind, and though less strict with my mother and myself, we lived in a very frugal manner. After his death I was informed by the family lawyer that he spent immense sums in anonymous donations for religious and charitable purposes. My mother died in the belief that he was a miser and had never done a benevolent action in his life,, He thought it right to conceal from her this giving of alms, and perhaps also he loved her more than he allowed her to suppose. But he did not make her very happy. Ah, what would have been my life without her! How often she caught me in her arms as I fled from the chamber of torture and kissed my bruised and bleeding hands! How often she soothed my wounded spirit with words of the tenderest love, and persuaded me to endure with patience the trials of my childish life! I did not then know that she suffered more than myself. She was ardent and romantic, fond of intellectual society, and not indifferent to admiration, possessed of remarkable beauty and many elegant accomplishments. But Harborne was a lone and sequestered village in the moors, and my father objected to social pleasures; so we received no visitors.

She had a heart which pined for affection; and he was a man of stone. She once told me that my birth had saved her from absolute despair: thenceforth she had something to live for, something to love. Often, as she pressed me to her bosom, she would gaze into my face with a timid, searching, craving look; and when with some cold words I tried to shake myself free, her deep, dark eyes would fill with tears. So it was also in your case, dear Ellen, and so no doubt you have found it with your little girl. Children cannot love us as we love them; and when they become old enough to return our affection, they leave us to marry or to make their way in the world. Happily it is good for us to love as it is good for us to labor, even when the reward is slight and inadequate.

My mother was a sad invalid, being afflicted with a pulmonary complaint which required constant attendance. The parish doctor saw her nearly every day, and received a fixed fee or salary per annum. Herbert Chalmers, whose name is yet remembered in science, was a student of promise and repute who had taken the cure of bodies in the parish of Harborne, partly for the sake of daily bread, and partly to study that particular phase of the profession. He had not been there more than a year when his friends obtained him a lucrative appointment. He thanked them and declined it, saying he was not ambitious and preferred living in the country. Now as the duties of a parish doctor combine in themselves all that is most unpleasant in the life of an apothecary's apprentice and the checkered existence of a post-boy, namely the rolling and pinching of innumerable pills, and long night-rides in the hardest of weather, his friends thought him out of his wits; but they could not change his resolution. Some time afterwards a relation died and left him a fortune. He built a mansion with a laboratory, hot- houses, and rooms suitable for collections and experiments, engaged a medical assistant, and devoted his time to scientific researches on the physiology and chemistry of the vegetable kingdom. But he still remained the doctor of the parish and attended all difficult cases himself. He reversed the usual order of things, for when he left a poor patient he slipped a guinea into his hand: that was the good doctor's idea of being humorous. His skill and unremitting care certainly prolonged my dear mother's life, though it could not save her from death at the early age of forty-three.

I had always been told from my boyhood that I was to be a clergyman; my father and mother both wished it, and I had no desire for any other profession. My college life was quite uneventful. I joined no set, indulged in none of the popular amusements, such as boating or cricket; and, living for the most part in my rooms, made neither enemies nor friends. I took a first class in Great Go, and the Bishop of T——, who ordained me, wrote a most kind letter to congratulate my father on the good examination I had passed in divinity. I preached my first sermon in Harborne Church; and though no one was there but our tenants and servants, my parents and the doctor, I did not dare raise my eyes from the book, and felt myself blushing two or three times as I read out some eloquent passages which I had composed in a state of exaltation, but which now seemed rather too fine for the occasion. However, my mother was delighted with this maiden composition, and felt very proud that I was ordained.

On Sundays, Dr. Chalmers always dined with us in the middle of the day; and that same afternoon we were strolling together in the garden — my mother, the doctor and I — when she said, "Well, doctor, you have not quite wasted your life in this dismal place; for you have made me live long enough to enjoy one day of perfect happiness." He made some reply which I do not remember, and then she said, "But tell me, dear doctor, I do not understand; why do you stay here when you might go to London and become the intimate friend of Davy, and Buckland, and the other great men with whom you correspond?" He answered, "That is my secret; and female curiosity cannot always be indulged." "Well, then, tell me.something else," she said. "Is it true you are going to be married? " He smiled and shook his head, and replied that it was not true. He was now forty- six years of age, and his day was gone. "Oh, doctor," she said, "you mustn't say that. Have you forgotten I am forty-three? Is my day gone too? " She drew herself up and looked very beautiful. Then she said, "You are still young enough, why do you not marry? Are you a woman hater? "Again he smiled, but this time I thought rather sadly, and said he was far from being that. "And do you not find it very lonely living in that great house by yourself? "Yes," he said, "it is very lonely." "And do you not sometimes feel unhappy?" "Yes, sometimes I feel very unhappy indeed." "And you do not think that if you were to marry ...?" "I cannot," he replied, "Is it for the same reason that prevented you from taking that appointment?" "Yes," he replied in a sharp voice, "it is the same reason." "Will you not tell me what it is?" (He shook his head.) "Ah, my dear friend, it would be better. You have something on your mind; will you not trust it to me? You have saved my life again and again; will you not let me prove my gratitude? Oh, disburden your heart, I beseech you. Edward, dear, leave us alone."

"No, sir," said he with emphasis, "do not go away." My mother thought that he was angry, and laid her hand upon his arm. I saw his lips turn pale, but he said in a firm voice, "Ellen Mordaunt, I thank you for your sympathy, but I cannot tell you this secret of my life, it would make you unhappy, and would give me no relief, but quite the contrary." He then shook hands with us both, and saying he was wanted at home, walked quickly towards the garden gate.

My mother looked after him, her eyes wide open with astonishment. I said there was a skeleton in every house. "Oh!" she cried, "Edward, what do you mean? He cannot have done anything wrong; that is impossible."

I did not reply, and we walked up and down the gravel walk. My mother seemed buried in thought. Suddenly she gave an exclamation and put her hand to her heart. She turned round and went a few steps as if to overtake the doctor, who had just reached the gate and paused there to look at us as he passed through. "Are you in pain, mother?" said I; "let me run after Dr. Chalmers?" "No," she cried earnestly, "do not call him back;" and seizing my hand she pressed it with convulsive force. I remained silent and lost in wonder, as she had been a moment before.

Then she said in her own quiet voice, "It was only a passing spasm, and Dr. Chalmers has other patients to attend. It is getting rather cold; I think we had better go in."

We went indoors, and my mother, complaining of a headache, retired to her room. The next morning I was awoke by the sun-beams streaming through the window. It was a fine spring morning, the birds in the garden were singing merrily. I felt in glorious health; the blood seemed to dance in my veins. Hitherto I had known no serious cares, and the troubles of childhood were past. A bright calm life was before me, and as I reflected on my happy condition my heart was filled with the love of God and with gratitude for his goodness.

One of the servants came in, gave me a letter, and hastened from the room. The letter was from my father. I have it before me now, yellow and crumpled and stained — written more than thirty years ago — yet still I weep as I read it.

"My son, I cannot see you to-day. It has pleased the Lord to chasten us with a heavy and sore affliction. Last night when I went to bed at a late hour your mother was asleep, but seemed to be dreaming. She turned from side to side, and was whispering something under her breath. I stooped down and listened, and heard her say the doctor's name. Then I feared that she was ill. Still sleeping, she flung her arms round my neck and awoke. When she saw me she gave a scream and shrank to the farther side of the bed. 'Wife,' I said, 'you have a fever; your face is flushed, and your hands are burning hot.; I will send James for the doctor at once.' I moved towards the bell, but she sprang from the bed and exclaimed, 'It is nothing, I am quite well, indeed I am; you must not send for him. Oh, do not send for him!' I saw that she was delirious, and rang the bell in spite of her feeble efforts to prevent me. Then she gave a great cry; the blood rushed from her lips and she fell to the floor. When I raised her in my arms she was dead."

Letter V

I REMAINED three months at home, and my father was very gentle and kind. One Sunday, as we stood side by side in the churchyard looking at the grave, he put his hand on my shoulder and said, "You were a good son to her." I noticed that his sermons were more humane, his mien and manners less austere; and I heard the coachman (an old servant) declare that "master was quite a changed man." But before I left home his old severity seemed to be returning.

The Bishop of T—— gave me a small living at Stilbroke in ——shire. The rectory being out of repair, I was invited by Mr. Jameson, apparently the squire, for his letter was dated Stilbroke Court, to stay at his house until my own was habitable. I accepted this invitation. A talkative neighbor on the coach told me that Mr. Jameson was a London tradesman retired from business, who about ten years ago had bought the manor of Stilbroke and set up as a country gentleman. "But," added my informant with a grin, and sinking his voice to a whisper, "the gentry don't call upon him, and he's not in the commission of the peace." He then went on to inform me that Mr. Jameson had one son, a lieutenant or captain in the Guards, and one daughter, who was lady of the house, her mother being dead. He said, "You'll find the bishop there spending the day; he's come down to consecrate a church." My companion then proceeded to elicit from me as much information respecting myself as I felt disposed to give him, and got down at a village near Stilbroke. I supposed he was a lawyer, or land agent, or something of that kind. I found Stilbroke Court a fine specimen of the old English manor-house, and Mr. Jameson, who came out of doors to welcome me, certainly seemed at first sight a fine specimen of the old English country gentleman. He wore a blue coat with brass buttons and a buff- colored waistcoat, and a snowy neck-cloth swathed round his throat. He had also a full-blooded, country-looking complexion; but when he spoke there was beneath a false accent of rusticity, a certain intonation which savored of the counter. I also observed in our first interview that he spoke with much hesitation, and made long stops between every phrase, the reason being, as I was afterwards able to infer, that on account of the bishop's presence he was leaving out the expletives with which he usually garnished his discourse. For when he first came down to Stilbroke, supposing that every country gentleman swore, he assiduously practiced the habit; and by the time he had discovered his mistake, the habit was acquired and could not be shaken off.

I felt some little trepidation when I found myself in the same room with the bishop. But Dr. Lambton came forward to meet me, and shook me warmly by the hand. Mr. Jameson asked me what I would have to eat, and resting his hands in a peculiar manner on the table, described the various dainties before him as if they were articles he wanted to sell. He was ... that is ... very glad to see me. Hoped I had a pleasant journey. Heard that the roads were ... extremely bad and heavy after the rain. Then I heard him mutter to himself, "Damn the damns, can't keep them down."

The bishop took me out for a walk in the grounds after lunch. He talked about my father and his own college days, described Oxford as it was in the last generation, gave me many practical hints respecting my parochial duties, and made me promise I would write to him as a friend if ever I required his advice.

He was to go away that afternoon, and we now saw the carriage driving round the sweep. Bidding me good-bye, he hastened to the house, and I walked along the gravel path, darkened by rain, to the end of the garden, where I found a little iron gate opening into a wood. But it was not an ordinary wood, being planted with many foreign trees, and bright with crimson rhododendrons. In other parts of the wilderness," as it was called, nature was left undisturbed; tiny little pathlets marked the "runs" of hares, and in thick patches of bramble were their "forms." The beech-mast of last year, brown twigs and dry leaves littered the ground, which was carpeted with moss and ribbed with the roots of trees. One charming little dell that I discovered was filled with blue-bells, more beautiful in color, I thought, than the flowers of the Himalaya shrub.

Brought up as I had been amidst desolate moors, it gave me an exquisite pleasure to walk in the shade of trees, to inhale their delicate fragrance, to view their dark pillar-like trunks and fair edifice of foliage. I stood on the brink of the dell and gazed down on the flowers like a blue lake lying in its depths. A few others of these wild hyacinths were growing singly or in clusters on the sides of the dell mingled with young ferns of the tenderest green, and one flower was growing at my feet. I had almost stepped upon it. A little way off, the sunlight descending through a window in the leafy roof flowed through the wood like a silvery stream, while around me the trunks of trees were flecked with patches of light. I heard a chirrup overhead and saw a squirrel leaping nimbly from branch to branch, running home to its young in the dusk, Sometimes the wind rustled faintly in the branches overhead and cast down raindrops shining like pearls as they fell. I was softened by these sweet influences. A tender melancholy stole upon me. A memory never long absent returned to my heart which was its home. Mine eyes streaming with tears fell on the hyacinth growing at my feet. I stooped down and caressed it with my hand. "Oh, delicate flower," I said, "your life is short enough and I will not pluck it from you; but if I could plant you in a garden where death and decay were unknown, then I would gather you at once. Thus God gathers beautiful souls; he loves them and takes them to himself. Dear mother, I weep not for you, but for myself; I know that you are happy, it is I — it is I who am forlorn."

I put my hand in my bosom and drew forth a locket, and pressed it to my lips. Mother, I said, send a ray of your love for me into some woman's heart that resembles your own, and so brighten my solitary life.

Then I lifted up my eyes and saw standing beside me a young lady of surpassing loveliness. She wore a white muslin dress of the kind which my mother used to wear; and from under her broad garden hat, long tresses of golden hair fell upon her shoulders. Her face had a grave and gentle expression which I know not how to describe, her complexion was pale, her eyes of a soft and liquid blue. Such was your mother when I first looked upon her. She was then only seventeen, the purest, the most affectionate of women, and one of the most unfortunate.

I rose and bowed; she shook hands as if we were friends. "Papa," she said, "sent me to call you."

We went towards the house; she made room for me in the narrow path to walk by her side. I furtively wiped the tears from my eyes. She blushed and said, "I fear, Mr. Mordaunt, that you are in much trouble?"

"My mother is dead," I replied; "and she was my only friend."

"Your only friend," she said timidly; "and your father?"

"I cannot love him," I answered, "so much as I wish;" and I gave a sigh. She sighed too. "Our parents," she said, "are our best friends, but sometimes —-" Then she checked herself and said, "Have you a sister?" "Ah, no," I replied, "if I had a sister then I should be happy, for I would make her live with me here."

"And what," she said a little more gaily, "what would you make your sister do — besides keeping house?"

"I would make her go with me to visit the poor and the sick — to tell you the truth, I am rather afraid of them — and she would teach me what to do. And then there would be someone who cared for me. It is hard to be alone in the world."

She did not reply. Her father took me over the village and gave me an account of my parish, prosing and swearing dreadfully. The next morning Miss Jameson came to me in the garden, followed by a maid carrying a covered basket on her arm. "Would you like," she said, "to be introduced to some of your parishioners?" I assented, of course, and enjoyed my second visit to the village more than the first. Margaret and I soon became intimate friends, and indeed almost like brother and sister. I stayed a month in the house, and when I went to live at the rectory our companionship was not interrupted. We were together all the day; and I almost reproached myself for being so happy a few months after my mother's death.

But about the middle of August the house was filled with guests, and Margaret's time was so taken up that we seldom saw each other alone. At the end of the month her brother came down with the Honorable William Fitzclarence, his friend. Captain Jameson was a sodden-faced dissolute-looking young man, with a carefully cultivated lisp and a vulgar laugh. He never pronounced the letter "r" except by inadvertence, and never replied to a question without screwing an eye-glass into his orbit, and surveying the other person through it with an air of mild astonishment, as if he had never seen him before. In short, he had taken the part of the dandy as his father had taken that of the country gentleman. In each case the impersonation was clever, which is all that can be said. Fitzclarence was a character. The heir to a peerage and a vast fortune, he was what was then called a "Philosophical Radical." He sat at the feet of James Mill, dined tete-a-tete with the famous Jeremy, and wrote for the 'Westminster Review.' He was one of the agitators for Reform, and was also reputed to be a violent hater of the Bible and the Church, a second Tom Paine. In those days a Radical aristocrat was almost unknown, and I really think he was the first of the species. The popular theory was that his head was turned, and certainly his manners were singular and his language often extravagant. As soon as he became excited in conversation he wriggled and writhed in his chair, and when he finished what he had to say, snapped his jaws sharply together like a dog at a fly. Though he disapproved of the game-laws he had a passion for shooting, and having quarrelled with all his relations, was induced by the fame of the Stilbroke turnip-fields to accept young Jameson's invitation. The other guests were mostly City people, and among them was an heiress to whom Mr. Jameson anxiously directed the attention of his son; for he was not enormously rich, and the captain was enormously extravagant.

One day when I was dining at the house the conversation turned at dessert, after the ladies had left the table, upon the recent discoveries in geology, which revealed the earth's antiquity and the creation of fish, reptiles, and quadrupeds in epochs separated by vast intervals of time. Fitzclarence expounded the matter with much lucidity, and each guest was apparently drawing his own conclusions for himself when Captain Jameson blurted out:

"Then the world was not made in six days. after all."

There was a dead silence, and all eyes were turned upon me. I said that the geologists must be mistaken if such was their theory, because it was clearly stated in the Bible that God had made the world in six days.

"Well then, Mr. Mordaunt," said Fitzclarence, "you do not agree with those of your brethren who declare that the six days in question were not actual days, but geological periods?

"How can they say that," I replied, "when each day is described as having an evening and morning, and when it is also said that God 'blessed the seventh day and sanctified it'?"

"Nothing," answered Fitzclarence, "could be proved more completely and concisely. We may, therefore, take it for granted that the six days of Genesis are not geological periods? "He looked at me with a questioning air. I bowed and smiled, and was going to change the conversation, when he said: "But now, if it were proved as an actual fact, beyond the shadow of a doubt, by the same kind of evidence as that which proves that the earth revolves round the sun — supposing, I say, it could be proved that the world was not made in six days, but that thousands and thousands of years intervened between, for example, the fish and birds of the fifth day, and man who was created on the sixth, what may I ask would you say then? "

"My dear sir," I replied, "you might as well ask what I would say if it could be proved that a circle is square."

But supposing it could be proved — please to answer for my argument's sake — what then?"

"Then," I replied, "of course it would be proved that the Bible was not inspired."

"Good," said Fitzclarence, rising from the table. "Well now, I will tell you this. It has been proved," And he walked out of the room.

Mr. Jameson poured forth a volley of oaths at his son for having set Fitz upon his hobby. The next day Fitzclarence wrote me a letter apologizing for his rudeness and begging me not to think of what he had said. The advice was kindly meant, but quite unnecessary; what he said seemed to me incredible, and it soon passed away from my mind. Not so, however, with the man. I observed that he gave up shooting and passed all the day at the house. Mr. Jameson, who knew my father to be rich, had always encouraged my visits, but now his manner was changed, and whenever we had any business to discuss, he was careful to make the appointment at the rectory. An infallible instinct warned me that Fitzclarence was my rival, and a gossiping servant confirmed it. My rival, I say, for now I discovered that I loved Margaret. So long as we were constantly together I was contented with her friendship; the days passed happily; I did not attempt to analyze my feelings; I did not reflect on the future. But, as soon as we were separated, my affection forced back upon itself became craving and intense. Unable to see her or speak with her as before, she became the constant companion of my thoughts. And now came the fear that I should lose her altogether. From my library window I could see into the Stilbroke grounds. Every day, at the same hour, they walked together on the terrarel he speaking with animated gestures, she listening with attention — no doubt with admiration. He was a noted orator, how could she resist his eloquence? Besides, he was heir to a peerage and her father was a tradesman.

Soon it was all over the village that they were engaged. A farmer told me the news, and declared Mr. Jameson himself had hinted as much to him, saying that before very long they'd hear wedding bells. Strange as it may seem, from that time I became more easy in my mind. It was a relief to be out of suspense, and now my duty lay clear before me; silence, self-conquest, resignation. I even smiled at the thought that perhaps I might have to marry them. At this time I read for the first time the 'Imitation of Jesus Christ,' and became enamored of the spiritual life. I resolved to place my happiness no more in earthly pleasures and human affections, but to seek only the divine love by purification of the soul, and fasting, and prayer, and exclusion of mundane thoughts. I resolved to banish Margaret from my mind and memory; when her vision forced itself upon me, I took up the 'Imitation' or the Bible. In the solitude of the night I found it hard to abstain from thinking of her, and I kept a taper burning opposite the bed to remind me of my resolution. I tied myself down in the chair to be prevented from going to the window at the time when she walked upon the terrace. In church I forbade myself to glance at the pew where she sat. My whole time was passed in idle devotion and selfish cares for the well-being of my soul. I almost ceased to visit my parishioners, and yearned to seclude myself wholly from the world.

A few months more and my ruin would have been complete. I should have become a mere God-fawning devotee. But this was not to be. Mr. Jameson called upon me one morning and said: "Come, parson, I say, you have dropped us. Won't you call over to-day and have a bit of lunch?"

I declined. "Ah," said he, "I know what it is. You don't like that infidel fellow; but he's gone away, and young Hopeful's gone with him. They had one day at the pheasants, that's all."

"What," said I, "Mr. Fitzclarence gone away! but, I thought —-"

"Ah, yes, you thought, and so did a good many more. But I'd never let my girl marry a damned infidel."

"Oh, please, Mr. Jameson, do not swear," said I.

"I am not swearing," said he. "I use the word ecclesiastically, just as you might in the pulpit; though it's enough to make anybody swear the way those fellows go on with their cursed atheism. Well, they'll find out their mistake some day. But you'll come, won't you? Let me tell Margaret you will."

I looked up at him. His little keen eyes were diving into mine. "My daughter," he said with emphasis, "will be very glad to see you; very glad to see you."

"I will come," said I. He went out, and I heard him chuckle as he went down stairs. There was little attempt at disguise in his words or his manner. Margaret was mine! At this thought the blood rushed from my heart and flamed on my pale ascetic face. I tore the hair shirt from my bosom. I dashed Thomas a Kempis on the flames. I knelt down and prayed. I jumped up and danced, exclaiming, "She is mine! She refused him for me! "As rivers, released from their bonds of ice, pour down swift torrents from the hills, so the natural feelings of my heart, so long held down by frozen piety, coursed swiftly through my frame and made me drunk with excitement and joy. However, I calmed down, and felt rather foolish as I took the 'Imitation,' all charred and smoking, from the fire. I remembered that, after all, nothing was certain as yet; and soon I became just as anxious as I had before been confident. It wanted an hour of the time, but I could not wait any longer and went up to the house. She was in the drawing-room alone. As I entered at the door I felt a strange faintness and fluttering within me. In a few minutes my fate would be decided. Her look reassured me, and the gentle pressure of her hand and the tone in which she said, "It is so long since I have seen you."

We conversed for some time. I feared to speak, and yet for my own peace of mind I knew it must be done that day, and that hour. At last I said with a bantering air, "Margaret, I hear that you have had an offer of marriage?" "Yes," she said with a smile, "and poor papa was so disappointed." "And why did you not marry him?" I asked. She blushed and turned her head aside. I took her hand in mine. "Tell me, dear Margaret," I whispered. She looked up, and told me with her eyes. Then I clasped her in my arms; I strained her to my breast; I pressed my lips to hers and fondled her long golden hair. Oh, raptures of a first and innocent love, who can describe them? What power have words to express the deep inner feelings of the heart? I can only tell you I was happy — that is all.

Letter VI

My father approved of the match and promised me a liberal allowance. The marriage was to take place in a twelvemonth. Captain Jameson did not deign to give us his blessing, being deeply offended with his sister for her refusal of Fitzclarence, for he preferred a brother-in-law with a handle to his name. His father's sentiments were not dissimilar, but he took the trouble to conceal them, having come to the conclusion that it would be foolish to refuse the heir to a large fortune because the heir to a still larger fortune and a peerage had been lost. So he was always loud and boisterous with me to show his cordiality. One day, at luncheon, he winked and said, "The bishop has a good opinion of you, Master Ned, a deuced good opinion of you."

I said I was glad to hear that I was so honored. No prelate was more loved in his diocese or more distinguished on the bench.

"Cannot you remember what he said, dear papa? asked Margaret, blushing with pleasure.

"I should rather think I could," he replied. "'Mr. Jameson,' said my Lord, 'Mr. Jameson,' said he, 'our young friend did well at college, damned well, and, by Jove, he'll do the right thing by your parish.'"

"Oh, papa!" exclaimed Margaret, "he could not have said that."

"Well, my dear," said her father, somewhat confused, "I don't mean to say he used those very words, but that was the general sense."

A servant came in with the letters of the afternoon post. Mr. Jameson's face fell as he examined the blue envelopes. "Ah!" muttered he, "I know what these are well enough. Reform — reform is all the cry. I wish they could pass a bill for reforming extravagant sons."

"You know, dearest Edward," said Margaret, as we walked to the rectory together, "Robert spends a great deal of money — papa would send him into the Guards — and we have heard that he gambles at Crockford's. And he is so dreadfully conceited; he would not even look at Miss Brown when she was here. His wife, he says, must have three things — birth, beauty, and money (or blunt, as he calls it). Now, as he has neither of the three to offer in return —-"

"But your father is rich?" said I. Margaret shook her head. "Papa," she said, "was in such a hurry to be a country gentleman that he gave up his business too soon, and though he is an excellent manager, and spends very little money on himself, he does not seem able to refuse Robert anything. The rents of the farms on the estate just cover our expenses down here, and I fear that papa's other money is going very fast. When he asked me to marry Fitzclarence, he said, 'My girl, you must not marry a poor man, for if at any future time you should want money, God only knows whether I should be able to assist you.'"

Dear Margaret, thought I, as I went up to my library, when we are married you will not need any money from your father. None of these sordid cares shall trouble your life.

I sat down in my arm-chair and abandoned myself to reverie. I had now found in love — chaste, secure, requited love — that calm of mind which I had sought in monkish devotion. No passion disturbed me; no disquietude alarmed me; no sad experience made me doubt my future happiness. I knew not the dangers of life. I pictured myself the rector of a large parish, and Margaret the queen of our world, distributing her bounty to the poor, alleviating their miserable lot. Often we had planned and plotted together how we could do good. And I saw her seated by my side after the labors of the day, and rosy-cheeked children clambered on my knees. And the love of my children unborn filled my heart, and I revelled in anticipated joys.

While thus I was wrapped in sweet meditation, I observed lying on the table before me a large brown-paper parcel which must have come down by the London coach that afternoon. I found that it contained Lyell's 'Principles of Geology,' and some other works upon that science. I supposed these were sent by the disappointed rival, and with no good intent; and as I turned over the books a letter dropped out. It was without an envelope, and as follows: —

DEAR YOUTH, — Here are the books you ask for, viz. the grand work of Lyell, and the orthodox attempts at a reply. Why on earth do you want them? Are you going to study these problems? If so, it would be better than some of your other occupations. I hear that you go very often to the top of St. James' Street. Ah, beware!

"Impossible to accept your invitation. I only go to Reform dinners nowadays. I talk, think, dream of nothing else. All is going on well: we are certain to succeed.

"Lastly, oblige me, once for all, by not writing as you do about a certain young lady. I admire her, I esteem her, I love her; it was my fault that she could not love me; but it eases my vanity to know that there was a prior attachment. — FITZ."

It was now evident that the books came from the captain, who had mislaid the letter in the parcel. I thought I could best disappoint his benevolent intentions by reading them carefully through; in fact, I had intended to order from London the latest works upon geology, as I considered it my duty to study the enemy's arguments in order to be able to refute them. I began to read the 'Principles' at once, and was soon captivated by the beauty of the style, the modesty of the author, and the wondrous world he opened to my view. There was not an allusion to theology in the book, which I read all through like a novel, with no sensation but that of enjoyment. But when I remembered afterwards the duration of time and absence of catastrophe on which it insisted, I was seriously troubled, and I read it again, now well on my guard, and in a hostile attitude of mind. But I could discern no flaw in the reasoning, and could only venture to hope that the facts were not to be relied on. Having spent a week upon the 'Principles,' taking many notes, and honestly forcing my brain to receive ideas it did not like (which I found at first very difficult), I took from the parcel an orthodox work which was then of much repute in the religious world. This book settled the matter in my mind: it was not unfairly written, admitted the facts which science had established, and tried to reconcile them with the Mosaic account of the creation. It was most ingenious — a perfect specimen of special pleading — but nevertheless could only deceive those who wished to be deceived: no doubt the author was among that number; I do not question his sincerity. There was also a pamphlet in the parcel, written by a clergyman, who allowed that the first chapter of Genesis could not be accepted as literal truth, but argued that it was of no consequence, as the Bible was intended to teach us religion, not to teach us geology. For me it was enough that there was one mistake in the Bible; that proved it could not have been written by God.

The next six months I devoted to biblical studies. I read the Bible all through, with no commentary but that of common sense, and the scales fell from my eyes. Never did I more keenly appreciate the beauties of the book as a literary production; but I found proofs in every page that it was written by men, and by men immersed in superstition. I passed many unhappy hours, for old beliefs are not torn up without a pang; but my chief feeling was one of burning shame, that I could ever have credited the many profane and ridiculous fables contained in the Bible. It seemed to me an awful blasphemy to assert that the great God of heaven clothed himself in the body of a man, and I prayed him to forgive me for having believed it. My conception of the Creator was ennobled, my devotion was increased, a pure and sublime Theism reconciled me to the loss of some illusions. Thus I did not suffer as much as might have been anticipated.

But I was a clergyman. I was the priest of what I now believed to be a pagan religion, and received money to teach what I knew to be false. I felt it incumbent upon me at once to leave the Church and to enter some other profession. Mr. Watson, the rector of the neighboring parish, frequently visited Stilbroke Court; his wife was a friend of Margaret's, and he, I knew, was a man of temperate views, who would patiently hear what I had to say and advise me how to carry out my resolution.

Letter VII

MR. WATSON had a large family, as was shown by the number of small caps and coats hanging up in the hall. I was ushered into an apartment which, like a desert island, bore no traces of human habitation. Everything remained as it had come from the hands of the upholsterer. The atmosphere was damp and cold, as if no fire had ever been lighted in the polished grate. The chairs and sofas looked as if they were in a shop-window; the gorgeous books on the central table had perhaps never been opened, certainly never been read. All feudal castles contained a dungeon in which malefactors were cast; and in many old-fashioned houses a desert chamber is set apart for the reception of guests. I did not like to sit down for fear I should crease something, and did not dare to walk about for fear of soiling the carpet; as it was, I could see a bootmark which the lady of the house would view with no less horror than Robinson Crusoe the footprint in the sand. I therefore remained in a most uncomfortable attitude, while the door was constantly opened by small children who peeped in and made faces at me, and then shut it with a bang and a shout of exultation. At last the rustle of a silk dress announced that the change of toilet was completed, and Mrs. Watson came into the room, round which she glanced with an air of evident pride. She begged me to sit down; but I said I was anxious to see Mr. Watson at once, so she led the way into his study, having made me promise that I would take a dish of tea before I went home. Soon afterwards I heard, not without satisfaction, the sound of manual punishment, accompanied by shouts which were not of a gleeful character.

Mr. Watson was seated in his study, reading Paley's 'Natural Theology' and smoking a long clay pipe. When I had explained the object of my visit, he did not seem surprised, but asked me a number of questions which showed that he was well acquainted with works of science and philosophy. Having received my replies, he reflected a little, and then said, laying down his pipe, "I see you have thought out this matter for yourself and have not taken it at second-hand. It would be useless for me to try and move you out of your position. I shall therefore place myself in that position; I shall admit (for argument's sake, you understand) that you have found out the truth. We shall, therefore, discuss what is best for you to do."

"Surely," I said, "there can be no doubt about that. I ought to act according to the truth."

"You think it is your duty to withdraw from the Church?"

"Most certainly," I answered, "and I have come here to ask your advice as to how to proceed in this difficult matter. I do not wish to cause scandal or to give unnecessary pain. But remaining in the Church is out of the question altogether."

"Gently, gently," he replied; "allow me to ask you what are your circumstances? What have you to live upon when you are married?"

"I inherit a sum of money from my mother, the interest of which is 150 pounds a year. That is my own. Besides that, my father has promised me a liberal allowance, and then there is the money I shall make."

"Perhaps your father may refuse to give you an allowance when he finds that you have left the Church. Is that quite impossible?"

A little reflection forced me to admit that it was not quite impossible; but, on the contrary, rather probable than otherwise. "However," said I, "that matters little; I am young, I will enter another profession, I will make my way in the world."

"You are not then aware," said Mr. Watson, that clergymen are forbidden by law to enter any other profession?" [This law has since been repealed.]

"Then," said I, nothing daunted, "I will get work from publishers and editors. I shall easily get on."

"Excuse me," he replied; "I have lived some years in London and have written for the press. Hundreds of indigent clergymen, many of whom are fine scholars, seek in vain for employment of that kind. The supply far exceeds the demand. No; look at the future fairly in the face and don't stir up a vague mist of hopes and illusions. If you leave the Church you cannot marry Margaret."

I was stupefied. Strange to say, I had never thought of this.

Mr. Watson did not interrupt my meditations, but quietly filled another pipe and began to smoke again. I said, "What do you advise?"

"I think," said he in a kind voice, "that I can show you are not bound by the moral law to give up the Church."

"Ah, sir," said I, "duty speaks to me clearly enough, though I have not, I feel it, the strength to obey its commands. I cannot part from Margaret. But I know that I ought."

"All moralists are agreed," he replied, "that the welfare of mankind is the test of the Right. The virtues so called are virtues because they contribute to human happiness. If they become injurious they cease to be virtues. Now life is so constituted that no positive dogma, no undeviating rule can be laid down for the guidance of conduct. In a broad sense, we may say it is for the welfare of mankind that everyone should speak the truth, but there are many exceptions to the rule. No one would hesitate to tell a lie in order to save the life of an innocent man. Here, as often happens, there is a choice between two evils, and the lesser evil is selected. It is wrong to tell a lie, but it

42

is more wrong to participate in murder. Or, if you please, we may put it another way. Here is a choice between two virtues. It is good to tell the truth, but far better to save an innocent life from destruction, while the struggle it costs the good man to lie adds to the nobleness of the deed.

"Having thus proved, as, I think you will allow, that there can be a case in which falsehood is a virtue, I will take a case which, from what I know of the clergy, happens, I imagine, very often. A parson with a wife and family of children entirely dependent upon him ceases to believe in the doctrines of the Anglican Church. His first impulse is to obey the voice of his conscience, and to leave the Church, but a little reflection warns him that if he did so his wife and children would starve. He chooses the lesser of two evils. He becomes, if you will, a hypocrite" — (here the pipe fell and broke into splinters on the hearth) —" that he may not violate the sacred duties of the husband and the father.

"And now, my dear Edward (if you will allow me so to call you), which, in your case, is the greater evil, and which is the less? If you were a man living alone and bound by no ties to another human heart; if your leaving the Church would only involve loss of money and social position, I would say, Be honest, be free! live on bread and water, work with your hands, break stones upon the road, rather than be untrue. But you are not alone; a life is entwined round yours like the ivy round that larch over there on the lawn. Margaret loves you. And consider how much harm you will do to others if you proclaim yourself an infidel; consider how much good you may do if you remain in the Church. You need never preach a doctrinal sermon; in the New Testament you will find maxims of the purest morality and precepts of the tenderest love. Let these be your texts. What does it matter, after all, if your parishioners believe in some fabulous legends of the East and some Greek definitions of the Undefinable? These are only intellectual errors. You are not surely like those theologians who maintain that an incorrect theory of the Universe involves eternal perdition. You believe in a life of future rewards and punishments, and it is in your power, as a clergyman, to convert men and women from a life of brutality and vice. Outside the Church you could do little; but, clothed with its authority, how much sin you might destroy, how much misery you might alleviate! Let this be your atonement, and it will not be refused — it will not be refused."

The good man's eyes were filled with tears, and he said as he pressed my hand: "Let us not speak of this again unless it is necessary for you. It is a painful subject for me."

We are easily won over by arguments to that which we secretly wish. That same evening I wrote to inform Mr. Watson that I had determined to take his advice, and, as he desired, would not allude to the matter again, I read no theological books, increased my devotional exercises, and spent the greater part of the day with the sick and the poor. Practicing the strictest economy, I was able to give away in charity all the money I received from the Church. Thus I quieted my conscience for a time — but only for a time. It was not with me a question of the moral law and of the duty of man to man. I was deeply, fervidly religious; and when I knelt down by my bedside at night to confess myself to God, when I reviewed my conduct of the day, I could not believe that it was pleasing in his sight. I felt myself a traitor to him — a coward, who paid outward allegiance to a false God and worshipped the true God in secret as if it were a sin. I felt that I was doing wrong. My conscience spoke in no uncertain voice. I could only sigh and weep, and pray God to have mercy on my weakness and forgive Me.

But I knew my own guilt in which I persevered, and I knew that I did not deserve to be forgiven. And in time there came upon me in these nightly prayers — often prolonged till the dawn — a conviction that God had turned his face away. For when I offered up my supplications, no response came back to my heart; that wondrous feeling of relief and consolation, the reflex action of the soul which rewards those who pray with intensity and faith, ceased to exist for me, and I rose from my knees unrefreshed. Yet when I thought of proclaiming the truth, of parting for ever from my love, I cried, "It is impossible!"

Now I began to suffer the most horrible torments. As I lay in bed unable to sleep, I saw lights dancing in the room and shadows passing to and fro; I heard groans and sobs, mingled with bursts of smothered laughter. One night I beheld my mother and Margaret in heaven, whilst I was borne past them by demons, and a voice cried aloud, "They believed in the false, but they were sincere. To you the truth was revealed and you hid it in your heart."

The Sunday I dreaded as a day of doom. The tolling of the bell seemed to summon me to the tortures of the rack. Often, when I was reading the lessons, I felt an almost uncontrollable impulse to throw down the Book and proclaim it a lie. Often, as I was preaching, voices whispered in my ear all kinds of blasphemous things, and sometimes I thought that I had repeated them, and, stopping short, would question the faces of the congregation to see if it were so. Ah, terrible days! even now it would give me pain to enter that church. I see it before me as if it were only yesterday — the white-washed walls, with texts in many-colored letters — the plain, open pews, and the people ranged in long rows — the window of crimson glass, and the sun-rays lying like blood streaks on the floor.

Margaret saw that I was ill and begged me to go to the seaside. She thought I had overworked myself among the poor; and, indeed, my labors were prodigious — but they had been a kind of relief. I did not take her advice, for I felt that I must make an end. Mr. Watson's arguments might be perfectly just, but in every great crisis of the mind it is feeling, not reason, that decides. Convinced that if I continued my life of falsehood and silence I should forfeit my eternal happiness, I resolved to seek security — even at the cost of Margaret. Again and again I sought her to tell the sad news, but when I came within the charm of her presence, I felt as if I could suffer anything, even the torments of the damned, rather than relinquish her love. Then, again, when I returned to my house, haunted by demons, I cursed my cowardice and swore that next time should be the last. But my confession was wrung from me by an accident.

One evening, Margaret and I strolled out after dinner to the wilderness. We went to the hyacinth dell; the flowers were as beautiful as ever; it was the same time of year. We stood on the spot where then we had met. I told her I thought at first she was an angel from my mother in heaven; and she said with a blush that she loved me from the first because I looked so pale and sad; pity made her take me to her heart. We spoke yet more of the past and revived tender memories; for a brief space I forgot the troubles that menaced our life.

We saw Margaret's maid tripping down the path which led from the village to the house. She held a letter in her hand, and said that as she was passing the post-office a gentleman's groom rode up and inquired the way to the rectory. When she found that he had a letter for me she took charge of it, thinking I would like to see it at once.

Margaret took the letter from her hand. "Oh, thank you, Jane," she said, "it is important indeed!" And she showed me the episcopal seal. Jane smiled and curtseyed and went on to the house.

I opened the letter, and we read it together. The bishop had heard of my labors, and was glad to say it was now in his power to give me a wider field. He offered me a parish in the county town with a salary of 800 pounds a year.

Margaret clapped her hands. "Oh," she said, "this is the high- road to fortune. You will be as great as you are good."

Then she stopped and looked at me in wonder.

"I cannot take it," I said; "I am an infidel."

She started back in horror, clasping her hands. She thought that I was mad.

"I have long concealed it from you," I said. "It is all over now. Dear Margaret, we must part — for ever."

She turned ashy pale and trembled all over.

"O Thou Divine Ruler," I cried, "eternal Spirit of Truth, for thee I have wounded this heart that I love more than all that is on earth. Give her strength to bear this affliction."

She sank on my breast and flung her arms round my neck. "Edward," she said, as she raised her haggard face towards mine, "Edward, I cannot give you up. I am still your betrothed. I will be your wife for better for worse, rich or poor, sinner or saint — what do I care? Without you I shall die."

"My child," I said, "the Almighty God has sent us here for a few short and unhappy years, not to do that which is pleasant, but that which is good, and to prepare for the life beyond the grave. You must not disobey your father; and he will never consent to our marriage. From this day I cease to be a clergyman."

"You do not love me," she cried.

"I do not love you, Margaret! Look at these sunken cheeks, these hollow eyes, these emaciated hands. Love and religion, love and honor have daily contended within me; see, have I not suffered?"

"And love has lost! love has lost!" she cried, and clung to me with her despairing arms. Not a tear dimmed her eyes, which were filled with and woe. "Edward," she whispered, "let us be silent; let us keep this dangerous secret for a time' Ah, I have a way. You are too ill to take a large parish. You are forced to travel for your health; but before you go we shall be married. Then we will live abroad for a long, long time; and then —"

"O God!" I cried in a loud voice, "preserve me!"

Her head drooped upon her bosom.

"Preserve us," I said, "from sin and hypocrisy."

She drew back and folded her trembling hands, pallid from violent emotion. "Command me," she said, "and I obey."

"Dear love," I said, "let us suffer on earth that we may be united hereafter, to part no more."

"Then, life, pass quickly," she said; "and come death, to make us meet again."

"As a perishable day," I said, "life will pass, and death will soon come to herald in the dawn."

I pressed her to my heart. The shades of evening descended, and the voices of the wilderness were hushed. The pale moon arose; the hours passed by. Twice, thrice, the great bell rang from the house; again and again we said farewell, again and again we flew back to each other's arms. At length we saw torches gleaming through the trees. One last kiss and she ran down the path to the house. I returned to the spot where first we had met, and gathered some flowers and put them in my breast.

Letter VIII

WHEN I returned home, I told the servants that particular business called me to London at once, and that I might perhaps not return for some little time. The whole night I was engaged in writing letters: to Margaret a long farewell; to Mr. Jamesod, a short note explaining my departure. I wrote to my father, gave my reasons for quitting the Church, and promised to write again as soon as I had a fixed address. I sent my cheque book to Mr. Watson, and begged him to pay the tradesmen, servants, &c., and to send my personal effects to an address which I would afterwards communicate. I also asked him to permit his curate to take my duty till someone should be sent by the bishop in my place. Having packed a small valise, which I carried in my hand, I walked down into the village a little before day break and posted the letters. Then I waited for the coach. The grey streaks of dawn were beginning to flushing into pink, the birds were twitter and to shake the dew from their plumage, laboring men were going to their work, when the horn sounded and the horses' hoofs rang sharply on the road. In a few minutes more I was borne swiftly away, looking back on a vanishing scene and lamenting the joys that were gone.

I took lodgings for a week at a market-town twenty miles from Stilbroke, on the London road. Thence I wrote two letters to the Bishop of T——; the first was a formal resignation of my living; in the other, which I marked "Private," I thanked him for his great kindness, and related at length the process of thought which had led to the change of my belief.

He wrote back the kindest letter possible, and told me how he himself, when at my age, had also passed through a period of skeptical gloom and had all but given up his profession. However, his doubts soon passed away and never returned to trouble him again. He advised me to travel on the Continent for a year, and before the twelvemonth was ended he had little doubt that I should have returned to my belief. In the meantime my interests should not suffer; he should consider my absence as sick leave; for he was sure that my brain was over-worked and that this attack of infidelity resulted from physical disease.

Return to my belief! As well might a river return to its source. My reply was respectfully, gratefully expressed; but it was conclusive.

This correspondence being ended, and Mr. Watson having sent me my clothes and books, nothing detained me in the town; and now I felt a yearning for home. I remembered what Margaret had said, that "our parents are our best friends." I remembered my father's kindness when last I was at Harborne, and the promptness with which he had consented to my marriage. I believed that, in spite of his cold exterior, he really loved me tenderly; and it was my duty to consult him before I began my new life. I thought of going to London; but if he wished me to stay with him I would obey.

As soon as I had made up my mind to go home, I felt too impatient to wait for a reply, and wrote word to say that I was coming by the next day's coach.

Harborne was not on the coaching road; and I alighted as usual at a wayside inn, about five miles from the village. The ostler took down my luggage and greeted me in the accents of the north, which sounded home-like to my ears. Presently I saw the dog-cart in the distance, and James drove up to the door. The horse had his water and hay, James had his beer, and I was just stepping up when he suddenly said, "Beg pardon, Master Eddard, I nearly forgot this here; "and he took a handkerchief out of his hat, and a letter out of the handkerchief. I read it with one foot still upon the step. It was from my father, who said that he could not receive in his house a hardened infidel; and that if I came in spite of his letter, he would turn me out in the presence of the servants.

I ordered the ostler to take out the luggage and carry it indoors. James became red in the face. "Bain't you coming home, sir?" said he. "No, James," said I; "my father and I have a quarrel it seems; but I daresay we shall make it up by and by." He touched his hat and slowly drove off. I inquired if a coach would again pass the house that day. They said that none would pass either way till the next morning at eight o'clock. I ordered a bed and some dinner, and then going up to my room locked the door.

I tried to eat something at dinner, for I knew that I had need of bodily strength; but it was impossible. The sight of food disgusted me. Feeling restless and excited, I went out of doors and walked quickly along a familiar path. A strong wind was blowing from the north; and across the moon sailed the clouds, tinged by its tawny halo and pierced by its cold white rays. Around me lay the moors like a wide black sea. On, on I walked, wailing aloud. At length I could give vent to my grief. Nobody could hear me. O miserable man! two sorrows had stricken me at once. I had lost my love; I had lost my home. I was an OUTCAST; alone and desolate. Then my blood boiled and my tears dried up; and I cursed my hard- hearted father who had put me to shame that day.

Lights twinkled in the distance. Harborne was before me. I skirted the village and climbed a steep hill lying on the left. The sky was now covered with clouds, and the wind was boisterous. A storm was coming up.

The church loomed before me mistily on the summit of the hill. I found that the gate was not locked, and entered the graveyard. Above the grass mounds and small stone slabs, a white obelisk rose; I fell on my knees before it, as before an altar, and prayed to God. I summoned the spirit of my mother from the past, and she to my memory vividly returned. Again I saw her face so loving and resigned; again I heard her sweet sad voice. And as I thought of the long years she had passed with a loveless man in a lonely house, and what she must have suffered, and how she had endured, I repented of my own poor rage and resolved that her life should be my example, and that never would I cherish an unkind thought against my father any more. For what pleasure had I left but that of being good?

The black night deepened, and still I remained kneeling by the tomb. But now the storm, which had long been gathering, burst forth; in a few minutes I was drenched to the skin, and the moist wind penetrated to my bones. I tried to shelter myself beneath the yew, but it creaked, and groaned, and swayed to and fro as if about to be torn from its roots. Then I crouched under the wall and fell into a stupefied sleep.

When I awoke, the storm had ceased, the sky had cleared, the moon, dull and red, was near the horizon. I knew that the dawn must be near, and that I must go back to the inn. But my limbs were cramped, I could scarcely stir, and my whole body was racked with pain. I dragged myself along on my hands and knees, and this movement partly restored my circulation. But to walk five miles! It seemed hardly possible. Yet done it must be, somehow or another.

At that moment I heard the sound of wheels. A man driving a gig stopped at the churchyard gate, and, having fastened the horses' reins to the post, walked slowly to my mother's tomb.

He bared his head and stood with his arms folded on his breast, gazing intently on the grave. Then he said in a low voice, Ellen! and turned to go away. I cried out his name and staggered towards him. He bore me in his arms to the gate, put me beside him in the gig, and drove at full gallop to his house. Having given me some brandy, he called two men and made them rub me with flesh- gloves from head to foot. But the next day I was delirious with fever.

Letter IX

AN overworked brain, a troubled heart, days of incessant anxiety, and nights without sleep were the true elements of my illness, and exposure to the storm but its proximate cause. Sooner or later it must have come; and I was fortunate in being cast like a waif by the winds into the house of Dr. Chalmers. He restored me to health; but I was in bed some weeks, and my convalescence was slow, though not tedious. For many it is a happy time, that period which lies between sickness and health. It has its own delicate enjoyments, such as the singing of a bird, the scent of a flower, the prospect of the blue sky, the mere sensation of being in the bright open air. The brain soon becomes weary, but a calm and soothing sleep at once relieves its fatigue. The selfishness of suffering is past; gratitude and love, which too often cease with convalescence, then at least animate even the coldest dispositions.

I used to sit for hours in an easy-chair watching the doctor as he performed chemical experiments, or made microscopic observations. When I had regained my health, I began the study of physical science; and in six months had made considerable progress, not only in the literature, but also in the practice, if I may use the expression, of astronomy, chemistry, botany, geology, and comparative anatomy.

But could Dr. Chalmers teach me all this? Was he a universal genius? The fact is that his house was a College of the Sciences. Since I had left home he had taken to live with him, besides his medical assistant, three scientific men whom he called his Professors. They were an astronomer, a geologist, and a comparative anatomist — all men of mature years who, having given up their lives to pure science, had found it difficult to live. Dr. Chalmers had plucked them out of poverty and had given them a home, only stipulating in return that they should work, and regularly publish the results of their researches. They were all delighted when I was presented to them as a pupil, and spared no pains to make me a proficient, each in turn privately assuring me that his science was the most important and the most interesting. I spent an hour or two with each of them every day.

The Anatomist inhabited a room built over the stables. On a large marble table usually lay some quaint-looking animal which he was dissecting; and round the room were arranged, in systematic order, the skeletons of the animal kingdom, culminating in a chimpanzee and a man, standing side by side, their arms affectionately interlocked. The Anatomist told me that his parents, who were poor, had sent him to Guy's Hospital. He had passed a good examination and had taken his diploma; but a visit to the Museum of the College of Surgeons sent him out of his senses; from that time he could think of nothing else but comparative anatomy; and Dr. Chalmers saved him from starvation.

The Geologist resided in a fine library, furnished with works on his science in English, German, and French, and colored maps and diagrams hung from the walls. He had a large cabinet filled with specimens of rocks, and of precious minerals in nests of cotton wool; and promised that when I had mastered these and read up the text-books he would give me lessons in field geology, and show me nature at work, and take me where I could study the "dip" of strata, and "faults," and other phenomena, which could be but imperfectly learnt from books. The Geologist had once been a laborer, and had taught himself to read and write. The finding of some fossils in a quarry "set him on to geology," which he studied after his day's work was done; and the rector of the parish, having a taste for the science, obtained him a situation in a small country museum. There he educated himself and continued his favorite pursuit; and there he was found by Dr. Chalmers, who offered him bed and board, and all his time to himself, and as much pocket-money as he might require.

The Astronomer had been an optician. He studied the sun and the moon and the stars from a tower at the end of the garden, with a small chamber at the top almost filled by an enormous telescope. The roof of the observatory was a dome in which was a fissure or window-like opening. The telescope being pointed towards that part of the sky which was to be the field of observation, a crank was turned, and the dome, which rested on cannon-balls in grooves, turned round till the window came opposite the telescope. On a table were papers covered with abstruse mathematical calculations.

The Professors met at dinner in the evening, and I found their conversation delightful and instructive. After dinner they went to the Common-room, as it was called, where they read the papers and the scientific periodicals. To these they contributed, but each Professor was also preparing a book, the labor of years, and the summary of a life's investigations. The Volcanoes of the Moon — the Natural Arrangement of Fossils — the Homologies of the Animal Kingdom, were the titles of these forthcoming works. Dr. Chalmers had already published a book on the chemistry of plants. He maintained that it was the duty of every student in science, history, and all other provinces of knowledge, to place on record in a permanent and accessible form the result of his research and experience. To amass knowledge, and to take it to the grave, was to be a miser of that which was to mankind more precious than gold. Such a person, however learned he might be, was utterly useless to his species; and the modesty which shrank from publication was in most cases an excessive vanity resembling disease.

He advised me to continue my general studies for some months more and then to select one science. He had little doubt that I would fix upon geology, in which case some knowledge of botany and comparative anatomy would be indispensable; and therefore my present work would not be thrown away.

I followed his advice and utilized my opportunities. But you must not think that Margaret was forgotten. If the virulence of my grief had abated, the dull aching pain yet remained. I told Dr. Chalmers how the ardor of the spiritual life had once enabled me to drive Margaret from my mind, and I asked him if he thought that devotion to science would have a similar effect.

"Why," said he, "do you wish to forget her? I should say, rather hallow and preserve her memory, place her image on the altar of your heart; believe that she is the witness and judge of your actions and your thoughts; then your life will be noble and pure. Love without hope, then your love will be to you as a religion, for none so nearly approaches the love that is divine."

These words, extravagant as they may seem, touched me deeply, for I knew that he had given up his life to a hopeless love which he had kept during long years chained down within his breast, as in a dungeon, and had fed it only with the bread of affliction and the water of tears.

However, I must proceed more quickly with my narrative. It was tacitly settled between the doctor and myself that I was always to stay at his house, and he also projected visits to London, geological excursions, and so forth. One day as I was passing through a shrubbery near the stable-yard (which overlooked the road), I heard James, who was in the dog-cart, talking with one of the doctor's grooms, and as they spoke very loud I soon discovered that my father was the subject of the conversation. He was like a mad dog, James said, when he heard that I was living with the doctor. He had taken the latter to task, James being present, and "had got as good as he gave, with sommat to spare; and he was that furious he'd ride over the moors and leap the stone walls rather than pass the doctor's house." This seemed to afford satisfaction to the servants, for my father was not universally beloved; but it was a sad blow for me. I felt that I must go. When I announced this resolution to my friend, he said I owed my father no duty since he had cast me off, I replied that still he was my father. He had brought me up, I had lived upon his bread, he had loved me so far as was in him to love, he had sacrificed to me many long hours, and had placed all his hopes in my gaining glory, or at least doing my duty in the Church. Those hopes I had shattered; the last half of his life I had embittered. It could not be helped; it was not my fault; but still so it was, and at least I ought not to cause him unnecessary pain. It would cost me much to go away, for I was very happy there; but my conscience left me no choice.

"Do you love your father?" inquired the doctor.

I answered without hesitation, "No."

"I," he said, "made a sacrifice for one whom I loved. But you can sacrifice yourself for one whom you do not love, and yet you say you are not a Christian."

"Because I have ceased to be a Christian," I replied, "that is to say, because I have ceased to believe in the Divinity of Christ, is that a reason for me to reject what is good in the teaching of a good man?"

Dr. Chalmers was much depressed by this determination; he loved me for myself, and not only for myself. Often I had observed his eyes fixed sadly and fondly on my face, in which he saw the features of one who was no more. However, in a few days something occurred which gave another channel to his thoughts.

He received a letter from my father, to the following effect: It was all over the country, that on the night of my arrival he (my father) had discovered in a secret drawer a packet of letters from Dr. Chalmers to my mother. Having read these letters, he showed them to me, and turned me out of doors; and I, of course, was adopted by the doctor. My father said that this mischievous tale would be kept alive so long as I remained where I was; he made no appeal to me, whom he looked upon as "lost," but if Dr. Chalmers cared for the reputation of a lady who could no longer defend herself, he would prove it by sending me away. He must see for himself that this abominable scandal had arisen wholly and solely from the fact of my being harbored in his house.

Dr. Chalmers at first declared that the story was a trick, but that I could not allow, for I knew that my father would never tell a lie. A few inquiries made through a trustworthy servant brought ample confirmation of the fact. It made a sad impression on the doctor's mind. "For a quarter of a century," he said, "I have lived with these people, and there is not one amongst them who has not received a personal kindness at my hands. She also was good to them all, and this is how they speak of us. Oh, poor human nature — poor human nature!"

He resolved to leave Harborne and never to see it again. Having placed the establishment under the charge of his housekeeper till he could make some permanent arrangements for the Professors, he went with me up to London. He declared that he would travel and explore the wild countries of the world, and seek in savage life that gratitude of which civilized men merely possess a shadowy remnant — the relic of primitive times. I may as well say at once that he was not very successful. At Mozambique he bought and set free a negro slave who stole his gold watch and decamped with a slave-hunting expedition into the interior. In Patagonia he rescued a wife from being half-murdered by her giant of a husband — in return for which she assisted with a hearty good-will her lord and master to belabor him. Lastly, he took up his abode in Brazil with a tribe of Bush Indians, who, having begged from him all that he had in his possession, stripped him of his clothes and turned him out of their camp as an idle vagabond who knew nothing of hunting or fishing and was not able to pay for his keep.

Letter X

BEFORE Dr. Chalmers left England he saw me embarked in my new profession — if such it can be called. He begged me to accept from him a small annuity, but I said my 150 pounds a year was almost sufficient for my wants, and the rest I ought to earn for myself. He then introduced me to his publishers, Jansen and Haines, in Paternoster Row. This firm, now extinct, was famous in its day for the publication of the classics; of original scientific works; of translations from the German; of lexicons, encyclopedias, annotated catalogues, and so forth. Now, my father had taught me German, on account of its value in "dogmatik," and the doctor had made me take it up again on account of its value in geology. French, and a little Italian, I had learnt from my mother. I had a general smattering of science, while the prima classes before my name in the University Calendar incontestably proved my classical learning and made a profound impression on the firm. Having first tested my capacity for work, they set me on their Paternoster Cyclopedia, which was rather out of date, to correct its errors and insert the latest additions to knowledge. As change of work is a species of repose, I was also employed to enlarge and improve a Greek lexicon which they had published for "the use of colleges and schools." I agreed to produce a stated quantity of "copy" per week, and they to pay me the sum of 3 pounds for the same. Thus I had now 300 pounds a year and was perfectly content. I took lodgings near the British Museum, in the reading-room of which my days were passed. It was not the magnificent hall I once took you to see — the paradise of learned loungers and spectacled flirts — but a dingy apartment frequented by none but genuine students.

At first I was obliged to work very hard and had not an hour to myself; but when I had hit upon a system, and learnt the art of reference, I was able to complete my appointed task at the Museum, and could study in the evening for my own pleasure and improvement. I must own that often I felt my existence lonely and monotonous. The days followed one another, and all, except Sundays, were the same. One evening, as I sat by my fire, I said to myself, "What a poor life is this, drudging from morning to night just to earn food, and lodgings, and clothes! You have no one to care for you, no one to converse with, no friend, not even an acquaintance. You say 'Good morning' to your landlady at the lodgings, and you make some remark about the weather to the man who takes charge of your umbrella at the Museum. You go once a week to Paternoster Row, hand your roll of manuscript across the counter, and receive three sovereigns in an envelope. Such are the social pleasures you enjoy; there is no place for you in the human family; years will pass, and your life will not change, and at length you will become an old man, and, unloved, unpitied, will go down with sorrow to the grave."

Then I felt sick at heart, and the tears rose to my eyes, and I thought of the happiness I had lost. "Oh! Margaret, dear Margaret!" I cried, "do you still remember? do you still lament? Do you weep for me as I weep for you? Does a vision haunt you sleeping and awake — by night a dream, by day a memory?

"Past are the joys of love, the thirsty kisses, and the long embrace; past are the hours of chaste converse and tender confidence; past are the hopes that once were all assured. None but Margaret can be my wife, and she for me is dead and buried in the grave. I must go through life solitary and alone; no pretty children will clamber on my knee. Alone — alone — alone. O God, my Father, and my Friend, you have poured love into my heart, and my nature is affectionate. Must I be lonely and childless? Is that, indeed, my destiny? Then, I pray you, assist me to bear life with patience to the end."

At that moment the servant brought in a copy of Mrs. Carter's 'Epictetus' which I had ordered at a book-shop that day as I was coming home. I opened it at hazard and began to read; and soon, as if by a magic spell, my pains were charmed away, my mind was filled with serene and elevated thoughts. Ah, what a divine gift is that which, by scattering some ink drops on paper, can, after two thousand years, still give solace to hearts in sickness and adversity! It is said that the ancient Egyptians placed over their public library this inscription, The medicine of the soul; and in all such melancholy hours as that I have described, I used to take up a great writer of the past or present time, and in half an hour my troubles were forgotten. It was this antidote to sorrow, and also my discipline of daily work, which saved me from brooding on my woes. I do not think that I loved Margaret less than she loved me; but I certainly suffered less, as I was soon to learn.

One day I met Mr. Jameson in New Oxford Street. To my surprise his face brightened up when he saw me, and he said, "Ah, here you are! I've been looking for you everywhere."

"Looking for me, Mr. Jameson," I repeated.

"Well, no," said he, "not exactly that; but I've been in London some time (Stilbroke is let), and I've been always expecting to see you in the theater saloons, or larking about at the Finish, or some of those places."

"And pray, sir," I asked, "why should you expect to find me in such scenes of dissipation?"

"Why, ain't you an infidel?" he said. "And don't they always knock about town? But there, I didn't mean to offend you. Why, you're as red as a turkey-cock! Is there any place handy where we can have a quiet bit of chat?"

I took him to my lodgings, which were small but comfortable. "Well," said he, "this is a snug little crib; and the Governor ain't cut up rough after all?

I explained to him what my circumstances were, and said that, "Thank God, I had as much money as I wanted."

"Thank God!" said he. "Then you do believe there's a God, after all?

"Certainly, I do."

"Well, then, you believe in the Bible too?

"No," said I; "not all of it."

"My dear fellow," he said, "you contradict yourself; for how can you believe in God and not believe in God's Word? But, then, never mind — that's not the point — that's not the point."

He walked up and down the room, muttering according to his wont when excited or disturbed. "Three hundred a year isn't much — but it's bread — it's bread. Will your father disinherit you, Mr. Edward, do you think?"

"That, I should say, was certain," I replied.

He went on, walking backwards and forwards, saying, "Bad, sir, bad; but it must be done; there's no choice — no choice."

I was much puzzled by this strange behavior, and the questions he asked, and his evident anxiety as he waited for my answers. Something rose within me, too vague to be called hope; a kind of expectation. Finally, Mr. Jameson put on his gloves and said, "I want to see you on particular business; will you call at ——'s Private Hotel in Half-Moon Street, at nine o'clock this evening."

I went there at nine o'clock, and was shown into a large, dimly-lighted drawing-room. A young woman came and advanced hastily towards me. It was Margaret's maid. "Please to sit down," said she, pointing to the sofa near which I was standing. "Jane," I said, "tell me ——" "Sit down, sir," said she. I sat down. "It is all right," she said with emphasis, "and Miss Margaret will be down directly." My head swam round and fell back on the pillow of the sofa. "So I thought," muttered the girl. "No, Jane," I said, "I have not fainted, but it was very near." "Bear up, sir," she said, "and be calm. Do not agitate my mistress; she is still very ill ——"

"What has happened?" I asked. "What has happened!" she said bitterly. "Why, what else could have happened! When you ran off like a thief in the night, Miss Margaret took ill; and since that day she has never laughed nor cried; and she never said a word, but just pined and pined away. And then the doctor and Mrs. Watson told her father that he must find you for her again or she would die. And he promised he would, and that made her hearten up a little. Oh! sir, be kind to her, for she's the best young lady in the world, and she's going to send me away because you can't afford her a maid; and my old mother's got only my wages to live on, or I'd serve her gladly for nothing. O dear!

I put a sovereign into her hand and said, "There, Jane, give that to your mother, or buy something pretty for yourself; and you must not mind leaving your mistress, for you will get married yourself before very long, I dare say."

This vulgar panacea for the woes of the lower classes seldom fails of its effect; and Jane wiped her eyes, smiled, dropped me a curtsey, and saying, "I wish you all happiness, sir, and many of them," went out of the room.

I waited. The moments seemed hours, and she did not come. The lamp burned dimly and cast vague shadows on the ceiling overhead. The fire crackled in the grate; the furniture creaked; hasty footsteps passed along the street; Piccadilly murmured in the distance. Why did she not come? Presentiments assailed me. Her father had changed his mind; she had fallen ill. A misfortune had happened. I cast myself in a chair by the fire and resigned myself to melancholy thoughts. Then suddenly something quivered through me like a flame. I felt that she was standing by my side.

But was this my beautiful Margaret? Pale and hollow were her cheeks, and the dress hung loosely on her wasted form. She looked at me sadly with her sweet blue eyes. I drew her towards me and kissed her pale and trembling lips. I took her on my knees and laid her head upon my breast. Thus she remained — sometimes uttering a sigh, sometimes nestling her head more closely to my bosom, as one who had been long weary and would sleep. Two hours glided by; the girl came in to take her to bed. I rose and said, "To-morrow." No other word passed between us in this meeting sad as a farewell.

Letter XI

AND this same sadness at first underlay our married life. I was perfectly content so far as my own lot was concerned; for me our marriage was all pure gain; I did my work as usual, and then, instead of the gloomy parlor of my bachelor days, I returned to a love-bright home. But it pained me to see that my wife was not happy; and yet how could it be otherwise? This was not the life of which we had spoken in the days of our betrothal; this lodging-house parlor and bedroom; this solitude and separation, I at the museum, she in utter loneliness. This it was which troubled her, not our poverty. She did not care for books, and was not a musician: she had no intellectual resources, and could not amuse herself when she was alone. As the wife of a curate she would have been in her proper sphere. She loved the sick and the poor, and all old people and children. She loved all who were helpless and in want, and spent much of her time by cottage bedsides, and by the arm-chairs of the aged placed out in the sun. But in London none of these kindly occupations came within her life; and she had no gossip with female acquaintances, none of those little gregarious pleasures which women think more of than men perhaps can understand. Then her health was shattered, and often I saw her looking mournfully on her thin neck and emaciated arms. Once only I alluded to her illness. She blushed, and hid her bead in my breast, and said that "only women knew how to love." Then she burst into tears. But save on this occasion I never saw her give way to sadness. I inferred rather than perceived the sorrow at her heart, for in my presence she was cheerful and vivacious. I gave up my book-hours, and read only now and then at odd moments: my evenings belonged to Margaret, and were spent in playing at chess, draughts, &c., or in conversation.

When you were born, my dear child, we found our lodgings rather small, for a baby takes up a good deal of room. But we determined not to increase our expenses, for we had no expectations from my father (who had not answered the letter in which I informed him of my marriage), nor from hers. The Guardsman continued his extravagance, till at last Mr. Jameson summoned up courage to declare that he should not have another farthing unless he sold out. Captain Jameson asked his father what a damned tradesman like him meant talking that way to an officer in Her Majesty's Guards, but finally the matter was compromised by his exchanging into a cavalry regiment.

I must now beg you to suppose that four years had elapsed since our marriage. I was engaged by Jansen and Haines in compiling notices of the "obscure names" in a Classical Dictionary, which was intended to supersede Lempriere, at that time alone in the field. Margaret was also engaged on a work of education. The arrival of Miss Ellen Mordaunt into our social circle was a most fortunate event: my dear wife had now all that she wished for; she was never lonely, being never alone; and was perfectly happy and contented. She often said if our life had few pleasures it had also few cares: and that if we were rich we should always be anxious and fretful about some trifle or another. And we had one very great pleasure. Every summer we spent a fortnight at Limmerleigh, on the East Coast. A lawyer from that little town, with his wife and daughter, once took the drawing-room floor in the house where we lodged, and we happened to make their acquaintance. They saw that Margaret was in delicate health, and suggested a trip to the seaside, and placed their house at our disposal for a fortnight, saying they should be glad to have someone there who would take care of the furniture, garden, &c. This same arrangement was repeated the next year and the next: the Irvines always went away for two or three weeks in the summer, and then we took our holiday.

One Sunday, Margaret came to me with her eyes cast down, and said, blushing a little, that she had a favor to ask: would I go to church with her that morning? I said that I would go to church with her as often as she pleased, and we always went together after that. Dear Margaret! she had secret hopes that I might be converted, and used to glance anxiously at me when the preacher alluded to infidelity. She was much perplexed by my long and fervent devotions in the morning and the evening; for she could not understand how one could worship God and yet not be a Christian. But we never discussed matters of religion.

Well, as I said, we had been four years married, and Margaret was happy. Then came the great calamity. Captain Jameson had soon obtained an evil reputation in his regiment. The passion for gambling of the last generation was already in its decline; and a man was looked upon with disfavor who carried dice in his pocket and held out a pack of cards like a pistol to everyone who called upon him at his quarters. Moreover, ugly stories got afloat; the colonel warned young cornets against him, and he withdrew from the Guards' club, not, it was said, without pressure from within. In fact, Captain Jameson was not only a thoroughly unscrupulous gambler, but also "tout" or agent to a famous West-End usurer, into whose toils he decayed many a young officer, receiving a commission on his ruin. This commission was so small, and the destruction of future prospects and happiness so great, that it was really like burning down a friend's house to roast an apple. But what did he care? He was one of those men who are quite insensible to the suffering they cause, and are never troubled with qualms of any kind either before or after an event. However, his career was suddenly brought to a close, and he involved others in his fall. A young subaltern was heavily in debt and wished to raise a large sum of money. His father was immensely rich, and Jameson having reported the case by letter to his principal, received his instructions. He told Lieutenant Smith (as I will call him) that he could have the 8000 pounds whenever he pleased; his note of hand would be sufficient; but, as it was pure speculation on the part of the people in London, it would have to be paid for accordingly. This, of course, the man of great expectations did not mind in the least, and asked Captain Jameson to go up to town and arrange the "transaction," giving him the note of hand and full authority to act on his behalf. Captain Jameson obtained the 8000 pounds and his commission, went to Crockford's to gamble with the latter, and lost it, and then lost the eight thousand pounds. Lieutenant Smith wisely wrote to his father, and confessed all, in consequence of which Captain Jameson shortly afterward wrote to his father and informed him that unless 8000 pounds were produced within a few days, the matter would go to the C.C.C. In other words, he would be charged with felony, arrested, tried, and no doubt transported for the same.

Mr. Jameson's late foreman, and the family lawyer, and myself held council together. It was found that Stilbroke had been sold; that Mr. Jameson no longer possessed eight thousand pounds, that the sale of his son's commission was not a sufficient addition, and that to make up that sum it would be necessary for me to contribute my stock of money in the funds. I did not hesitate for a moment; my wife's family was mine, and the sacrifice was made. A few days afterwards, the Jamesons, father and son, the foreman and I met together at the lawyer's in Lincoln's Inn Fields. It had been made a stipulation with the captain that he should emigrate, and measures had been taken to prevent him from evading this arrangement. The lawyer read out the accounts. "Then there is nothing left over?" said the foreman. "Only this twenty-pound note which will pay for Captain Jameson's passage to Australia and buy him a rope when he gets there," said the lawyer. "Or perhaps the colony will save him that expense."

Captain Jameson took the money and retired. Mr. Jameson looked from one to another with a bewildered air. "Did you say there was nothing left, Mr. Lawyer; nothing left of all that money I earned? I worked hard for it, gentlemen. I was up early and late. I never wasted an hour. I was honest in all my dealings. Yes, yes; poor Bob has spent it all." Then he looked round at us again. "How," said he, "am I to live?"

I was, of course, prepared with an answer to this question, and had taken a bedroom for him at home. But the foreman said, "Come, my dear, kind old master; come and live with me." Then he turned to me and said, "Excuse me, sir, for taking your place; but you have done enough." He rose and went out, and my poor father-in-law tottered after him, holding his hand. He died in a few months; and Captain Jameson was shot in a gambling-house in Sydney, soon after his arrival, for something equivalent to what is called "welching" on the Turf.

It would have been better, perhaps, to have kept our money and left him to his fate; and yet, I am sure, we acted on the right principle. For he might have reformed; he might have become an honest, hard-working man, and even acquired a fortune. In novels, the air of australia has a wonderfully restorative effect on the characters of emigrants; and sometimes, no doubt, it is so in real life. Margaret said that he had great natural ability, and he must have had some qualities to make him the friend of Fitzclarence. But the passion for play quickly depraves a man; what are the pleasures of society or culture to those who have sat knee-deep in cards, and played night and day without intermission? Gambling is the most dangerous of vices, because its excitements are incomparable, and are followed by no reaction; it ruins, but it does not satiate.

We now lived from hand to mouth, but I was not alarmed; and there seemed no reason for alarm. Thousands of married persons were in a position not less precarious; it was, in fact, the ordinary lot. I was earning 150 pounds a year, and knew I could get copying and translating to do, for such work had been offered to me by other readers at the Museum. And, in fact, before long I was fully employed. But the work was miserably paid and was often required in haste. My evenings were no longer devoted to Margaret. I had to write — write — write from morning to midnight, or even to the following dawn. Thus, by immense efforts, I was able to make two pounds a week. When job-work was slack I tried my hand at literary composition, and wrote about twenty essays on social and literary subjects, which I dropped into Editor's boxes; but none of them ever appeared in print, so I confined myself to the manual labor of the scribe. We were still fifty pounds short of our previous income, and Margaret had to practice the mean little arts of economy, the saving and hashing the scraps of one meal for another, and so forth. I hate extravagance and waste; but it seems to me that this kind of thrift is apt to make the mind sordid and money paramount. "My dear," said I to her one day, "there are two kinds of poverty. When we had 300 pounds a year, if we had taken a house, we should have found it difficult to make both ends meet. But you were content with these bachelor lodgings and money never troubled us. In one sense of the word we were poor; but, as a matter of fact, we lived easily on a small scale. Well, now we are poor; our regular expenses are too much for our income, and so we have to scrape and stint in little matters, and think of pennies at every hour of the day. We have lost 50 pounds a year, and ought to reduce our expenses by living in a more humble way. At first we may find it hard to give up those little comforts to which we have been long accustomed; but habit will soon make us happy without them, and there will be an end to all this petty trouble and anxiety."

Margaret had grown fond of our dingy rooms and was sorry to leave them. It was there we had spent our honeymoon, and there you were born. However, she assented at once, as she did to all that I proposed; but a misfortune postponed our departure, and then rendered it no longer a question of choice and free-will. Alas! I had said there were two kinds of poverty. We had soon to learn by terrible experience that there were other kinds, the horrors of which may not be, cannot be, fully described. A part only of the truth I shall unfold.

Letter XII

As I told you, I read and wrote all day, and the greater part of the night as well. My night-work was mostly copying, and I made the mistake of writing on white paper, which is very trying to the eyes; I was also employed for some time copying manuscripts in a private library, and this work taxed my eyesight severely. I found that when I woke up in the morning, my eyelids were glued together, and a young doctor, whose acquaintance I had made at the reading-room, observing them to be watery and bloodshot, advised me to give them rest for a month. But how could I pass a month without doing any work, unless we could pass it without eating any food? I hoped for the best and worked on as before; and the consequences may be imagined. The next time I caught cold it flew to my eyes, inflammation set in, and a few days afterwards I was sightless.

My employers were exceedingly kind. They sent me ten pounds on account and begged me not to be anxious. I always did my work honestly and well, and they would not lose me on any account. They would find a substitute while I was ill, and as soon as I had recovered my health, there was my place ready for me. Unluckily, I twice returned to my work too soon (money was so needful to us), and twice I relapsed. This caused the firm much inconvenience and threw my eyes into a bad state. The disease assumed a chronic form, and a great oculist whom I consulted, said that time, rest, country air, nourishing food, and attention to the general health were the only medicines he could recommend.

Margaret had a good deal of jewellery, chiefly presents from her father. This we were now forced to sell, and obtained what we thought a considerable sum. We felt quite confident, that before it was spent my health would be restored, and went to live near Hempstead Heath where we found board and lodging at a very reasonable rate. But my eyes became worse, and, returning to London, we took a bedroom near the hospital at Charing Cross, for which I had procured an out-patient's ticket. There my case received every attention; but, as the oculist had predicted, medicines did me no good. Our money being now nearly at an end, we migrated to the neighborhood of Islington, where we took a garret at four shillings a week. We spent little money, but none came in; and, slowly, slowly our store decreased, till at last it was finished altogether. Hitherto, my dearest wife had alleviated the sorrows of my blindness by reading to me from my favorite books, but now they had to go too. I got very little for them, but we lived on the money two weeks.

"Dear Edward," said my wife, "you must let me write to your father, or our poor little Elly will starve." I gave my consent, of course, and she wrote; but no answer was received. We made inquiries about Dr. Chalmers. He had gone on a canoe voyage up the Amazon and had not been heard of for a year.

On my left hand I wore a gold ring, which my mother had made me promise always to wear in memory of her; but I thought that our destitution released me from this promise to the dead. However, I would not sell it; I would only pawn it, and within a year's time I should surely be able to redeem it.

One evening at dusk I went out and walked backwards and forwards before several pawnbroker's shops; but they were all too public — too near the crowded thoroughfare. At last I saw some way off, down a narrow side-street the three golden balls branching out from the wall of a house. This I thought was the place for me; so taking off my green shade, for fear of being conspicuous, and looking anxiously around me, though I only knew two or three persons in London, I slipped in at the door, which was invitingly ajar. I found inside three small doors, which opened into cells or private boxes with partitions on either side, so that those who stood before the counter could not see one another.

The shop-man was talking in a jocular manner to a woman in the box on my left; and having tied up her bundle of linen, put it on a shelf, pinned a ticket to it, and handed her the duplicate, he wished her good-day, and came to me. I handed him the ring, and he took it to the light, examined it carefully, and offered to advance me two pounds. I said that would do very well, as I only wanted the money for a few days. As I made this very foolish speech a tall thin young man in the box on my right stretched himself half over the counter and looked round into my box with a derisive expression on his face. The next evening I saw him talking to some girls before a public-house, with his white hat cocked on one side and a cigar in his mouth. There, thought I is a Captain Jameson of low degree, and perhaps he too has ruined his relations.

I learnt before long to go to the pawnbrokers without shame, and even to bargain with the shop-man. Little by little everything went — our boxes, our clothes — nearly all we had except what we wore. For the first time we were in debt; we owed a week's rent. The landlady came to us, and said "she saw we couldn't pay the rent, and she wouldn't demand it. But she'd got an old lodger come back who wanted our room, and so out we must go. There was his portmantle down-stairs, and him waiting in her parlor, We must foot it at once."

The little we had was soon made into a bundle, which I tied to a stick, as I had seen tramps do in the country. Your mother took you in her arms, and so we went out into the street.

It was the month of November. A fine drizzly rain filled the air, and covered the pavement with a layer of damp in which the gaslights were reflected. We walked eastward, keeping close to the houses on the right-hand side, for the street was thronged with men going home from the City. What a heartless crowd it seemed to us poor exiles of happiness, outcasts from humanity. There was scarcely a woman among them. They had pale resolute faces, and walked as fast as they were able, looking neither to the right nor to the left. Weary of being jolted and pushed, we sank under a doorway and watched them go by. An elderly man, poorly but neatly dressed, noticed us as he passed; he went on a few steps, paused, hesitated, then returned, put a penny in my hand, and went quickly away. We bought a roll, which we divided into three equal parts. It was the first time we had eaten that day.

The street grew empty, as it seemed, of a sudden, and we continued our journey. We made you walk a little now and then, and carried you by turns. Margaret insisted on this, though scarcely able to bear your weight. For a long time past she had been in failing health, and I knew she must be feeling very ill; but she said not a word in complaint. Sometimes she gently pressed my hand; sometimes I put my arm round her waist and gave her a kiss. Our love was greater than our misery.

We were now in the heart of the City, and it resembled a city of the dead. The streets that in day teemed with human beings were silent and deserted.

In the midst of these vast solitudes we felt like travellers lost in a wilderness of stone. We sat down and rested for a while. Then Margaret said, "Dear Edward, my courage faints. Will you pray with me?"

"No, Margaret," I answered, "I pray no more, God is hard- hearted."

"Edward! Edward!" she cried with a gesture of affright, "do not put such thoughts into my heart; they come there often, and I drive them away. Oh! my dear husband, make me good; help me to place my trust in God, and to love him, and to —-

Her words ended in sobs.

I embraced her and knelt on the cold stones. But I did it only of my love for her. I was sullen and rebellious. She knelt also, and prayed aloud with the sleeping child in her arms.

A policeman came up while thus we were engaged and told us to move on. I laughed a mocking laugh to myself. Yet my wife, was cheered by this hasty prayer and her eyes brightened up. When we had gone a little way she stopped and said, "Edward, it is useless to walk about like this; we can sleep in the workhouse, and that is better than being out of doors."

I had thought of this and feared to propose it, but it was no time for sentiment and pride. I saw a man coming towards us, and when he drew near it was plain that he belonged to the class who could give poor vagrants information and advice. He wore a fur cap on his head and a white comforter round his throat; he slouched along with his hands in the pockets of his corduroy trousers and was whistling a tune. I asked him if he could direct us to the nearest workhouse, where we might sleep. "Well," said he, "you won't get much sleep in them institutions. Why won't you go to a model lodging-house? It's only a penny a night, and every luxury of the season." I replied that we had not so much as a penny. "God strike me dead!" said he, catching up my hand, and feeling the tips of my fingers; "you're gentlefolk, too, by your hand". "We were," said I, "a long time ago." "I dare say now," said he in a coaxing voice, "as you were a clerk or something of that?" "Yes," said I, "not exactly a clerk, but doing the same kind of work." "And when your eyes went bad," he said, glancing at my green shade, "they gave you the sack?" I nodded. "And then you spouted all you'd got, except what's there in your bundle, and I don't think it's much, and you got behind hand with your rent, and they turned you out into the streets?"

I told him he had guessed right.

"Guessed I" said this man learned in misery, "it ain't guessing at all. Can't I see it before me just as plain as a play-bill on the wall? Now come along with me, and I'll give you a night's lodging and a bit of hot supper into the bargain. I'm flush, for I've just done a good bit of work. Don't trouble, sir; I'll carry the young'un."

"I suppose," said I, "that you are a skilled working-man."

Yes," he replied, "there ain't a skilleder man than me in my own line — bar one. I began life as a policeman, but I saw the error of my ways, and left off making war on my fellow-creatures what never done me any harm."

I asked several other questions, and he returned answers which I did not always understand, and which seemed intended chiefly for his own amusement, as he chuckled to himself after he had made them. He took us beyond the Bank, into a part of London where I had never been before. I saw to my astonishment a great wide street lined on both sides of the way with innumerable trays or trucks of fruit, fish, and other edibles, each truck being lighted by a candle in a glass shade. The pavement was crowded with people, all of the lower class, and the bustle was extraordinary. Our companion told us that this was the Whitechapel Road, and seeing that Margaret and I were both very weak, he bought us a penny cup of coffee. This gave us new strength, and we were able to keep up with him, though he walked very quickly, glancing from side to side and sometimes looking back over his shoulder. He said that it was against his principles, as a respectable working man, to dawdle in the streets; then he had such a large acquaintance in the Force, he feared he might perhaps be detained if he met any of them.

"Lor' bless you," said he, "they wouldn't let me go. I might tell 'em I'd got particular business, or that my old mother was anxious if I stopped out late, or that I was taking home friends to supper — they wouldn't listen to a word. They're so wary pressing in their invitations, are my old pals, they won't take no refusal, not at any price whatever." He now left the Whitechapel Road, and, turning to the right, plunged us into a perfect labyrinth of by-streets and alleys. Some of these streets were deserted like those in the City, and we passed two large buildings, each of which perfumed the air for a considerable distance; the first was a sugar bakery, the second a brewery, which last our guide sniffed with much satisfaction. One street we entered was devoted to festivity. Nearly every house was brilliantly lighted, and from half-open doors proceeded the sounds of harp and fiddle and thumping of feet; or laughter, clamor, and song. Women without any bonnets strolled to and fro, and half-drunken sailors rollicked merrily along. Not far from this street we came to another, in which the houses were all more or less dilapidated, and most of them seemed to be empty. The man told us we were "nearly there," and, giving a long shrill whistle, stopped to listen as if for a reply. Two whistles responded from the bottom of the street. He then pushed quickly on, passed under an arch into a small court, and, knocking at the door of a house within, called for a light. An old woman opened the door with a farthing dip in her hand, and the man having chucked her under the chin, and asked her if she felt pretty bobbish, led us up to a room on the second floor. It was a poor bare room enough, the walls blackened with dirt, the broken window-panes stuffed with rags; but it was a sweet refuge to us that night after our weary wanderings. Our host told us the old woman was his mother, and we mustn't mind her being cross, she being a real good sort all the same. He went out and talked with her some time. At first her voice sounded keen and shrill, but it softened down, and she came in with a mattress and blanket, which she laid on the floor, then served us some sausages, with potatoes backed in their skins.

After we had supped, our host came in and sat with us, smoking a short clay pipe. I was now able to study his appearance. On his right hand was a fresh red scar which he tried to keep covered with his left. It seemed like the bite of a dog. The expression of his face was not prepossessing. His look was kind, but it was askant, and there was something cunning in his smile. When he paid us little acts of attention, such as arranging the mattress, or making up the fire, it was done, so I thought, in an underhanded kind of way. However, I stopped myself in the midst of these reflections, which were not very grateful, and thanked him warmly for having saved us from the miseries of the street. He mumbled something about a workhouse being no place for her — pointing at my wife with his thumb.

I observed a heap of tools in the Corner of the room, and made some remark about them. He at once became vivacious and talkative as he was in the street, and his eyes twinkled in a most

75

singular manner as he spoke. "You see," said he, "I'm in the patent lock and key line. Now, here is a little inwention of my own." He showed me a leaden hammer capped with leather. "What d'ye think it's for? I'll tell you. Gentlemen often loses the keys of their patent safes, and then they send to the shop and ask for a man to open 'em. Of course they don't send the safe, 'cos it's full of gold and bank-notes. Well, it's no good trying to pick a patent lock; so the safe has to be opened by force with a wedge and a hammer. Now, I needn't tell you, gentlemen don't like a noise being made in their house like a blacksmith's shop; it wakes up the baby, sets the dogs barking, and alarms the neighborhood. So I inments this leather cap hammer, and it drives the wedge in without making any noise."

"I suppose you have taken out a patent?" said I.

"Well, no," said he, "I ain't done that — not ex-act-ly. But it's been the means of putting money in my pocket all the same. There's Jem Black what works with me, he goes to the Hall of Science and cultiwates his mind; and he says to me, 'Thomas, that's a beautiful inwention; Thomas, I'm proud of you; Thomas, you're a benefactor of our specie.'"

He now left us to ourselves, taking the tools with him, and in the morning gave us a breakfast of tea, and bacon, and eggs. In the midst of the meal a man rushed into the room and whispered something in his ear. I heard the word "peached." Our host sprang up, wrung me by the hand, and hastened out followed by his friend. In the afternoon the old woman came in. She was crying. She said, "We should never see her son any more." I asked her why. She only shook her head and covered her face with her apron, and rocked herself to and fro. After a time she went out.

A sergeant of police came in with two constables and searched the room. I now began to understand, and asked if the man who lived there had been taken up. The sergeant looked at me with some surprise and said, "Yes; burglary with violence."

The old woman left the house, and no one disturbed us in our occupation of the room. We lived chiefly on dry bread, which I begged from servants and at bakers' shops. I never begged for money, at Margaret's earnest request. Thus we were kept from actual starvation; but my poor wife became weaker and weaker every day. Then came a hard frost. We had no fire, and when I felt the keen air streaming in at the window, I knew that it would kill her. She lay with her eyes fixed upon me, trembling and shivering, yet pressing you to her bosom, chafing your hands and bare feet, while you cried in a weak, plaintive voice, "Poor Elly! so hungry, so cold!

Oh, Edward," she said, "if I could only have some tea; I think it would save me."

I went first to a large coal-yard, and picked up the pieces which were lying in the street near the gate, and put them in a cloth I had brought with me for that purpose. A gentleman who was coming out of the yard stopped and said, "Are you so poor that you can't afford to buy coals this terrible weather?"

"I cannot even buy food," I answered; "and my wife is dying."

"You have a gentleman's voice," said he.

"I was once a clergyman."

"I have known many cases of this kind," he replied, "and excuse my saying so; the cause has been always the same — drink."

"In my case," said I, "it was something you may think worse — Infidelity. Then followed sickness from overwork, doubtless a judgment you would call it. These eyes failed me, and they fail me still, or I should be at work."

"Well," said he, "I dare say I can find you something to do which won't try your eyes. Meet me here to-morrow at the same hour, and in the meantime take this for immediate necessities." He gave me a five-pound note and stepped into a brougham, which was out of sight before I had recovered from my astonishment. It causes me a pang even now when I think of that broken appointment. Why it was broken he never could know, and must have supposed I was drinking the money. Perhaps (who can tell?) it may have set him against being charitable any more.

I went to a grocer's and changed the note. I almost feared he would say it was a bad one, for the luck seemed too great to be true. I bought some tea and some coals and wood, and borrowed a tea-pot and mug from the people in the house. Margaret seemed to be asleep. I would not wake her till the tea was quite ready; then I would put the mattress close down by the fire; and when she had finished her tea, I would go to the cook-shop and buy her some good strong soup.

Her eyes opened; I sat down beside her on the floor, and told her the good news. She smiled; then her face changed in a curious manner; she put up her lips to be kissed like a child before it goes to sleep, and expired.

I sat there without moving. The dusky shadows were falling on the floor when a hand was placed upon my shoulder. I looked round. It was a City Missionary whom I had often seen passing from house to house; but he had never been to my room before. "My brother," he said, "you are in affliction."

I started to my feet. "There has been murder done here," I cried.

"What," said he, turning pale, "do you suspect ——"

"God has murdered her," I said. "The God who made her, the God whom she loved and faithfully obeyed."

He looked softly into my furious eyes and said, Do you think, then, that she is dead? No, dear friend, she is but released from this poor tenement of clay, and now lives with God in paradise."

"And could not," I cried, "could not this benevolent God make her happy in another world without inflicting these horrible tortures upon her? Look at that body, once so beautiful, battered and beaten by its maker. And it is not only her body he has wounded. If her soul could be made visible, it would show the marks of many a cruel and savage blow."

"Oh, silence these angry thoughts," he said, "and be resigned to the will of God. For he is our sovereign and our Lord; it is he who has made us and not we ourselves; we are his people, and the sheep of his pasture. My friend, let me implore you to humble your heart and kneel with me before the throne."

"What," I cried, with anger redoubled, "pray to that monster, that demon, that fiend! Think you that I, like a grovelling hound, will lick the hand that strikes without mercy and without provocation? Think you I am as the base Oriental slave, who presses the bowstring to his lips and to his brow? Think you that I fear his malignant rage? Hear me, bloodthirsty tyrant of the skies, you have power, and can rack me with everlasting pains. But I curse you, I defy you ... murderer ... fiend ... "

The foam fell from my mouth on my hands. I saw the missionary running from the room. Then I swooned and fell senseless to the ground.

When I came to myself I was still alone. I went to the window and looked out. Snow was failing heavily, and already the roofs of the houses were white. I listened to the roar of the streets. I pondered on my misery; and I thought of the black river which I had once crossed on such a night. The bridge was lonely I remembered. Few people passed by, and their footsteps could be heard from afar. But again fierce wrath rose within me; and I cried with a loud voice, "God, you shall not conquer me; I will fight out my life to its natural end."

Then a tiny little hand was put into mine, and a little voice said in a pleading tone, "Papa, why do you talk so angry and loud? you will wake up mamma. And you never look at Elly to-day. Poor Elly! so hungry, so cold!"

Then I was stricken with shame and self-disgust. I had let my poor child starve whilst I was ranting idly at the clouds.

I took out a handful of coins. "O thou vile dross!" I cried, "thou canst not give true happiness, yet without thee is misery and death. See, Elly, here is some money to play with, and I will go out and buy you something nice."

Your eyes sparkled — we all love money by instinct — and you took the silver in your lap. I knelt down beside the inanimate body, and asked it in a whisper to forgive me, for I felt that with my foolish rage I had profaned the presence of the dead. Presently you ran to me with a frightened face and pushed the money into my hands.

A number of men and women were standing behind me, looking sadly on the corpse. Then they led me away to another room. Thieves and prostitutes did the last offices of love for the body of my poor Margaret.

Letter XII

WHEN I awoke from sleep — a sleep, as I thought, of many dreams — I was in the room where Margaret had died. But her body was not there. The sun was shining brightly, the window was open, and the air that came in was balmy and warm. I sat up and looked out; there was no snow on the ground; flowers were blooming in a box on the sill, and a lark was singing in a cage fastened to the wall outside.

This I could not understand; besides, I was lying in a bed placed under the window. How had it come there? I glanced round the room. It was furnished. There was a plain deal table and several

80

rush-bottomed chairs, and cups and saucers, dishes and plates in shelves, and a kitchen dresser; and signs of cooking in the grate. I lay back in bed and tried to collect my thoughts.

The door opened, and two young women came in.

"If you please," said I.

"Hark, Sal, he speaks!" said one of them. "Lord! I feel 'most afraid."

"Oh, you fool! said the other; and coming towards me she drew a chair up to the bedside. Well, sir?" she cried.

"Where is the — Where is Margaret?" I asked.

"She was buried long ago," said the girl.

"Long ago! it was only last night that it happened. How can you talk to me like that?

"Hush, hush," she said, in a soft soothing voice; "listen to me while I tell you. That was three months gone by, and all that time you've been very ill. Then it was winter — cold, snowy winter. Don't you remember? And now it is the spring. Feel the warm air coming in at the window; hear the lark singing, smell the sweet flowers, see the blue sky.,)

Then those were not dreams after all, those days and nights that had followed one another, those faces I had seen, those voices I had heard.

"Where is she buried?" I asked.

She held up her finger. "You must not speak of that or your illness will come back."

"Tell me then, who are you?" I said, "and who is that girl over there?"

81

"We belong to him as brought you here. She is my sister, and we live in this and in another room. But now you're well you shall have this one to yourself."

"I believe," said I, "that you have saved my life." Her eyes became full of tenderness. "Yes," she said, "I have saved your life." Then she put her hand in her pocket. "The parson gave me this for you as soon as you got well."

It was a New Testament. "But I cannot read," said I. "Try it," said she, smiling. I opened and read without difficulty; my sight was restored! One malady had destroyed the other. I uttered an exclamation of delight. At the same moment the other girl who had gone out of the room a few moments before, brought you in, very nicely dressed, and your golden hair carefully combed out. "Kiss your papa, Elly," said the girl named Sarah, "he knows you now." Then, as she turned to go, she said, "If you think you owe me anything, please do not fret yourself ill, and ask me no questions about myself or my sister."

In a few days I was able to walk about, and tried to obtain some employment. But my appearance did not recommend me, for I was in rags, and my toes protruded from my boots. However, I called upon a law-stationer who was attracted rather than repelled by my evident poverty. This worthy man, as his shopman afterwards informed me, employed by preference persons in a state of utter destitution, as he usually found them not only grateful for his kindness, but also willing to work on very moderate terms. Having inspected my calligraphy (I had learned to write clerk's hand), he feared it would not do, but just as I was going from the shop, called me back and offered to pay me so much a folio — half the regulation price — which I accepted gladly enough. I wrote to Jansen and Haines, and said that my eyesight being now perfectly restored, I hoped they would allow me to resume my connection with the firm. I gave the law-stationer's as an address, and the publishers replied by return of post, that they had made arrangements with another gentleman in respect to the Classical Dictionary, but as soon as they had an opportunity, they would gladly avail themselves of my valuable services, and would lose no time in communicating with me.

No one would tell me where Margaret was buried, for they feared it might cause a relapse if I went to her grave. And I never found it out, for we changed our name when we went to live at the thief's house. Margaret was buried under the name we had assumed, and I could not remember it after my illness. On the day of my recovery, I told Sarah that my name was Mordaunt, and this trifling circumstance shaped out my future destiny by giving a clue to those who were in search.

I will tell you a strange thing. My illness caused by the passion of grief had swallowed up and absorbed that grief to itself. I did not mourn for Margaret, and almost rejoiced that she was taken from a life so full of suffering and pain. Now, the object of my life was to save you from such trials as she had undergone. I would work hard, and restore you to that position in which your parents had been born.

The day after I received the letter from Jansen and Haines, as I was standing near the door of the house, three whistles sounded, or rather shrieked, in the street outside. At once there was great commotion in the court. Several men dashed into their houses, and then emerging through the skylights, ran nimbly over the roofs. Those who were not frightened were inquisitive, and crowded to the windows and doors. The cause of all this stir was a middle-aged man with a fresh-colored face and yellowish whiskers streaked with grey. As he came into the court an old man (who had probably retired from business) went up to him and said, "Is anybody wanted?

"No," said the other; "private inquiry." Then be glanced at my face, and gave me a letter addressed Edward Mordaunt, Esq. "That is for you, sir, I think," said he.

This letter was from my father's lawyer, who informed me that Mr. Mordaunt was travelling abroad when my wife's letter was written: he replied to it when he came back, and as we had changed our address, his reply was returned by the Dead Letter Post Office. Mr. Mordaunt had then instructed him (the lawyer) to find out where I was, but all inquiries had failed, till at last a detective had heard of a person named Mordaunt living in the thieves' quarter, Whitechapel, and ascertained that the person in question was a gentleman by birth and answered to my description. Mr. Mordaunt, on receiving this information, was grieved, but not surprised to find that my infidel opinions had led me to adopt a career of crime, and that, having defied the laws of God, I should now set myself in opposition to the laws of man. In order to save a soul from perdition he was willing to adopt his grandchild, on the understanding that I made no attempt to see her again; and so long as I adhered to this condition be would pay me an annuity equal to that which I had squandered.

I said that I would consider the matter, and send a reply in a few days. I felt it was my duty to think of nothing else but your own welfare and happiness. I should endeavor to silence my affection for you since that affection would be a vice if it persuaded me to sacrifice your future. In my hands was your fate; what a terrible responsibility! If I could earn for myself a respectable position you would, I thought, have a happier childhood, and grow up a better woman than if educated by that austere old man. But was it in my power to escape from this kennel of crime? That morning the state of my eyes had given me cause for alarm, and in my weak state of health overwork might soon set them wrong again. Breathing a pestiferous air, living on insufficient food, it was not likely that I should regain my full strength, and without it I was doomed to remain in my prison- house. Before I went free I had debts to pay — debts which would never be claimed and could never be forgotten. After much thought I came to this determination. The next morning I would call upon the publishers, and tell them how I was situated, and ask them for pity's sake to give me a helping hand, not in the way of charity, but of employment. If they refused, then you should go; and though I feared your life would not be a happy one, at least you would not be brought up in a den of thieves.

I obtained on hire a suit of black clothes, which, though threadbare and worm-eaten, were better than the rags I usually wore.

As I stooped down to kiss you before I left the house, I could not refrain from tears. "Oh, my beloved child," I said, "they will take you from me and I shall never see you again. They will tell you that I am a wicked man, and teach you to hate and despise me. My darling, it is hard to give you up; but I must — I must — if it is for your good."

The tears rolled down my cheeks, and you took out your little handkerchief and wiped them away. I put on my hat. Then you said you would go too, and without waiting for an answer put on your things and thrust your hand into mine. "And why," thought I, "should I not take her? It may be our last day together." So off we went, through alleys and by-ways, into the Whitechapel Road, and past the Bank towards St. Paul's. It was a bright sunny morning, and the streets, I thought, were even more crowded than usual. Many a hard-featured man of business turned back to look at the pretty child perched upon my arm, her blue eyes bright with excitement, her hair shining like gold in the sun. I entered the well-known shop in Paternoster Row, and said I wished to see Mr. Haines on particular business. The clerk gave a start of recognition, then coldly said he feared Mr. Haines was out, but would go and see. My heart sank. Perhaps I might not be able to obtain an interview.

At that moment I saw the Bishop of T—- at the other end of the shop, turning over the pages of a new book. I felt my lips quiver. You observed it, and said in a clear shrill voice, "Do not cry again, dear papa, do not cry again." The bishop looked up from his book, and then bending over the counter asked a question of the clerk. I heard the words, "poor scholar ... used to do work for the firm." The bishop came towards me with a face full of benevolence and compassion. When our eyes met he cried, "What! Do I see Mr. Mordaunt?"

"Yes, my lord," I replied, "I am that unfortunate man."

He took me by the hand, and, pressing it kindly in his, led me to the chair where he had been seated; but the clerk, with an obsequious bow, showed us into an office like an old-fashioned pew; a kind of box with wooden sides and a railing round the top; inside, a desk and two stools. I told the good bishop all that had happened since I left Stilbroke. He listened attentively to my narrative, and said, "Wait here a little while, and I will see Mr. Haines: I am sure he will give you something to do." Then, having paused for a moment, he said, "Understand, Mr. Mordaunt, I do not sympathies with your opinions; they are most hateful to me; but your distress ——" He put his hand to his heart, and said, "it has gone in here." He stooped down and kissed you, and hurried from the office. That was the last time we met, for in after-days he always avoided me, and I did not force myself upon him; but often I have gone to the House of Lords to have the pleasure of looking on the face of my dear benefactor.

In a quarter of an hour I was called up to Mr. Haines' room. He appeared rather confused, but I did not think him to blame for his answer to my last letter. A publisher's is a house of business, not a charitable institution. "Mr. Mordaunt," he said, his Lordship has just asked me to provide you with some literary work, and I am happy to say that it is in my power to do so. We have been commissioned by a client of ours, who is something of a connoisseur in the classics, to bring out an edition of Thucydides, with critical notes. He wishes it put into good hands, and the bishop assures us that you have the requisite scholarship; besides, we know that you took a first-class at Oxford, a fact which speaks for itself. The editor is to receive three hundred pounds, and here" (handing me a cheque) "is a hundred in advance. But we make this stipulation, that you go into the country for the full space of three months and take a complete rest, that your system may recover its tone. It is easy to see that you are still far from being well, and if you begin work too soon we shall have the old trouble over again. So we make this condition on behalf of the —-, of our client. At the end of three months we shall expect you to return and prepare the work for the following book-season. And now I wish you a pleasant holiday, and shall be glad to hear how you are getting on whenever you are able to write me a line."

It was, of course, easy enough to understand whence came this shower of gold; but I did not trouble the bishop with a letter of thanks. I thought that the best way of showing my gratitude was to follow his instructions, and to edit the work in such a manner as to give him satisfaction.

Having cashed the cheque, I went back with you to the court in Whitechapel. Sarah was seated by the fire in my room cooking our dinner. I told her I was going, and had come back with Ellen to wish her good-bye. At the same time I gave her some money to repay her for what she had spent during my illness, and also wrote down an address to which she could apply whenever she was in need of any more. She took the notes with an air of indifference and thrust them into the bosom of her dress.

"Sarah," said I, "you saved me from death, and now I can save you from something as bad. Will you come with me and take care of Elly, and be a good girl?"

Her eyes brightened for a moment. Then she turned to the fire. "No," said she, "I mustn't leave Jem; it's only me keeps him from the drink."

She would not speak another word or even shake hands; and when you kissed her she turned her head impatiently aside.

Ah! who can understand a woman's heart? Who could tell by that cold set face what feelings were surging in her bosom? I have not said much about this girl, for there was bad in her as well as good, as many a robbed, half-murdered sailor had discovered to his cost; and I knew that any attempt to reclaim her would probably fail. But I also knew she would never do you any harm; that I could judge of from the past.

I have not described her character in full; nor have I described in full the horrible life of that White-chapel court. But I have shown — for it was my duty in justice and gratitude to show — that even in that sink of iniquity, even amongst those degraded and ferocious beings there were hearts full of compassion and eager to soccer the distressed.

That same afternoon I bought from the clothes-man a suit of the most gentlemanly garments he possessed; they had rather a marine aspect, but that did not so much matter, as we were going to the seaside. I redeemed my mother's ring and some trifles that had belonged to Margaret, and bought back some of my books (dear old companions and friends) which had not been disposed of I also had you dressed out like a fine little lady, and started for Limmerleigh that same afternoon.

Thus ended the days of my adversity.

Letter XIV

MY first month at Limmerleigh was spent in a state of unalloyed delight. To see innocent faces, to breathe the fresh air, was pleasure enough for one who had been imprisoned so long in a den of crime, a dungeon of disease. My strength was rapidly restored, and new blood flowed through my veins, as sap in dry trees when the winter is past. But my brain having recovered its vigor, forced me to remember and reflect. I was in the midst of scenes hallowed and endeared by the memory of Margaret. I thought of all her virtues, her piety, and love. I had never known her to be angry or cold, and she bore the most terrible calamities with cheerfulness and courage. When I came home to our hideous garret in Whitechapel, I found the same affectionate welcome as in the days of our prosperity; and when I gave her the scraps of dry bread which I had begged, she took them joyfully and jestingly, as if it were a feast. She once said that she thought Jesus and his disciples must have lived like ourselves, because it was in the Lord's Prayer, "Give us this day our daily bread;" and this fancy invested for her with a halo of romance our miserable lives. Her trust in God seldom wavered, but seemed to be strengthened by affliction, and the more she suffered the more she loved. My nature was not so submissive, and though now the spirit of foolish and impotent wrath had passed away — though now the old habit of devotion was knocking at the door of my heart — though now I longed to worship God, it was necessary first I should be able to revere him. I considered that if he were omnipotent, the death of Margaret was a crime; but from this painful conclusion I took refuge in a theory I had seen somewhere suggested, that God was perfectly benevolent, and had made the world as well as he was able, but that his power was contracted and controlled by the evil nature of the material with which he had to deal. This gave me comfort for a time, but I soon saw through the fallacy. For since men have been upon the earth they have made it better; and therefore, before they came upon the earth, God could have made it better had he pleased. If not, man is more powerful than God, which is contrary to reason.

But the opposite theory brought me to an equally ludicrous dilemma. For no man, if endowed with miraculous power, his moral nature being left unchanged, would be guilty of making a world in which murder is as the mainspring to a watch. Therefore man is more good than God, which again is absurd.

I now began to suspect that our conception of God was entirely erroneous. For what is the definition of God? A Perfect Mind. And what is Mind? It is a product of the earth, a created thing, existing within the lower animals in a rudimentary condition, and in truth not less human than the body. Mind cannot create, it can only arrange and dispose, as Shelley remarked long ago. Even a perfect mind could not create a grain of sand. We suppose that God is a mind, or has a mind, because mind is the highest species of force with which we are acquainted; and if we must define God, it is the best definition of which the human intellect is capable. But is it for man to define God? Is it probable that we who are but as animalcules crawling on a speck of matter floating in space — an infinitesimal fraction of the Universe — is it probable that we should be able to form from our minds a correct image of the Creator?

At this time I happened to read the well-known passage in Bacon's 'Advancement of Learning' — " Certain it is that God worketh nothing in nature except by second causes"; and this set me thinking on all that I had read in scientific works about natural law governing physical phenomena; and thence I was taken on to the conclusion that all moral phenomena and events are also subject to fixed and invariable law; that God has no personal relations with the earth; and that his entity or being is higher than a perfect mind, and far beyond human comprehension. But perhaps some clue might be obtained to the intentions of God in regard to ourselves by a careful study of the natural laws which govern the earth, as these laws, which for brevity's sake I shall sometimes call Nature, may fairly be considered the expression of his Will.

My friends, the Irvines, had left Limmerleigh, and their villa was for sale. One day I entered the garden, where I had passed so many delightful hours. It was now quite neglected. The lawn was strewed with brown and yellow leaves; the shrubberies were ragged and wild; weeds covered the gravel paths and the well-known flower-beds, which once were splendid with color and delicious with perfume. Everything bore the impress of decay. I went to Margaret's favorite rose-bush; it was dead! Alas! thought I, the same cruel law pervades the whole animated kingdom. Trees and flowers, insects and birds, the fish of the sea, the beasts of the earth — all must die, as men die, after a life of combat and pain.

Then I considered this fact from another point of view. Was it not strange that Man, who is God's "noblest work," should be subject to the same law as the lower animals, to the same law even as the flower? Was it not strange that Nature should treat the greatest men with the same unconcern as the meanest creatures of the soil, slaying wit a breath of pestilence a genius over his noble work, as she sweeps away with a breath of wind a spider spinning in its web? The injustice of this law, and its imperfection, troubled me exceedingly. After much thought I found the solution of the problem; but it was a sad discovery.

We are not sent upon the earth to pass through an ordeal, and to be rewarded or punished in another world, after death, according to our actions. We are sent upon the earth for the sake of the earth. In common with the atoms of water and air, we are part of the material with which the Creator, through secondary laws, carries out his scheme, whatever it may be. Those laws are evil and imperfect to us as they are to the insects and the flowers, but they were not arranged for our approval and convenience, and are no doubt perfect as regards the purpose for which they were designed.

This made me very sad. I reasoned with myself that it was but a theory; yet I felt it was the truth, and it forced itself upon me in spite of the aversion it provoked. I was humbled and mortified. So then we were merely as slaves, merely as lower animals, merely as potters' clay! And where now was the hope of a life beyond the grave? It is the best argument in favor of a future life that man deserves compensation for unmerited suffering; but if man is only raw material that hope falls to the ground. Then again the spirit of science spoke within me. "It is probable that in death the mind is decomposed (nothing is ever destroyed), and that its elements are recombined into other forms of mental life, so that though the individual intellect perishes, nothing is lost to the race. If this supposition be correct, great men bequeath not only their works but their minds to Humanity."

One soft June night I went out and sat on a cliff overhanging the seashore. The voices of the hay-reapers working by moonlight mingled with the sound of the waves breaking on the beach. On the west, dark pine woods lined the horizon; on the east lay the grey ocean; above was a cloudless sky, shining with innumerable stars, each Star a sun, the center and sovereign of a system. My head swam as, gazing upwards, I beheld worlds lying as thickly together as leaves in a forest — at least so it seemed; we know that in reality vast distances divide them. Oh, prodigious universe! I sighed. And oh, poor, vain, ignorant man, that could believe all these were made for him. Low indeed is our true condition in this wondrous galaxy of worlds. We call ourselves God's "noblest work," but perhaps there are in those distant orbs, or rather in the planets by which they are attended, beings who would look upon us as we look upon the ants and the bees; to whom our highest efforts of mind would seem but as curious instincts or faint gleams of rudimentary intelligence.

At that moment a gun was fired from the sea; the reapers came running to the brink of the cliff; and a great ship passed, gliding through the waters against wind and tide, its chimney of flame casting sparks into the air. It was the first steamer I had seen, and I rejoiced at this triumph of Art over Nature. Ha! ha! thought I, if man is small in relation to the Universe, he is great in relation to the Earth. He abbreviates distance and time, and brings the nations together. He covers the wilderness with cities, and cornfields, and gardens. He modifies climate and dispels disease. In every generation he makes the world happier and better than it was before.

I sprang to my feet and walked quickly to and fro. My brain was in a whirl. I saw the light again, the blessed light of hope and joy. "If we," I exclaimed, "are fellow-slaves with the humblest creatures of the earth, and even with the elements, we are also fellow-workers with God, and assistants of his inscrutable designs. For it is plain that one part of the Divine Scheme is the progress of the earth from a lair of wild beasts and savages to a paradise of happiness and virtue, and that Man has been selected to represent the good, to extinguish the evil; to be the Ormuzd that shall conquer Ahriman; to master by the powers of his intellect those laws of which he is now the subject and the slave."

And I believed that when Man fully understood and realized his mission, a new religion would animate his life. It would be a religious duty to battle with the evil in Nature and to labor for the glory of the planet, since for that purpose men were placed by God upon the earth. The intellect would be carefully trained; idleness and ignorance would be stigmatized as sins. The social affections would be developed to the fullest extent, and all men would abandon the hopes of personal immortality as a selfish craving at variance with the general welfare of the race. Having cast aside these personal desires, they would labor for posterity, and look forward with chivalrous delight to the bliss that others would enjoy.

Then I cast aside all thought for the future fate of my own soul. To labor and love without hope of requital or reward, what religion could be more pure and more sublime? Hitherto I had looked on the Earth as a strange country, and life as the journey of a traveller. But now the Earth became my fatherland, and all mankind my fellow-countrymen. I kissed the grass and flowers growing on the brink of the cliff; I sang to the waters, and the winds, and the beasts, and the birds, saying, "Together we accomplish the work of the Creator." And then — smile at me Ellen if you will — I felt a rapture of love for the whole human race. I resolved to preach the New Gospel far and wide, and proclaim the glorious mission of mankind.

This dream of prophecy did not last beyond the night. However, I had discovered a religion for myself; never since have I been distressed by the problems of existence; and I then laid down a rule of life to which I have always rigidly adhered.

My time at Limmerleigh being now at an end, I returned to London and worked at the Thucydides, which was received with much favor at both Universities. Henceforth I was a known man, and Mr. Haines, who was alone in the firm, and advanced in years, offered me a situation, with a fair prospect of becoming junior partner. Then Dr. Chalmers returned from the uttermost ends of the earth, took up his abode in town, and made me live with him. He published his notes on the Flora of the countries he had visited, and was made a Fellow of the Royal Society. He gave Sunday evening receptions, at which I had the pleasure of meeting nearly all the great men of science, and many distinguished authors and artists.

All urged him to prepare his Narrative for publication; but he had begun to travel too late in life; the book was beyond his strength; and the dear noble-hearted man died in my arms only three years after his return.

Shortly afterwards my father also died. He left the bulk of his fortune to various Christian missions for the conversion of India, as some compensation to the natives of that country for the exactions and oppressions of his father, the Nabob, when Resident at the court of Goruckpore. My name was not mentioned in the will; but the Hollywood estate was entailed, and therefore came into my hands. Had I known this, Margaret's life would have been saved; but I did not even know that there was such an estate in existence. I was informed by James, whom I now took into my service (or rather I gave him a pension), that my father's health, in spite of his iron constitution, had quite broken down of late years. Something seemed to be preying on his mind, and ten years before his death he left Harborne altogether. I believe that he loved me in his heart, and suffered like another Brutus. But what else could he have done? He acted rightly according to his barbarous Calvinistic creed. In his eyes I was a servant of Satan; and he refused me admission to his house, as he believed that God would refuse me admission to heaven when I died. Such is Faith! It is not only opposed to Reason, but to Charity; and with an unnatural piety can tear the fibers of a father's heart and leave him wounded to languish and to die. It was the perfection of his belief that led to so much misery.

If I were a young man endowed with literary powers, and about to begin my career, I should adopt as the work of my life the Diffusion of Doubt; for doubt dissipates superstition and softens the rancor of religious life. Without doubt there can be no tolerance, and the history of tolerance is the history of doubt. The skepticism spread by Voltaire humanized the dogmas of the Roman Church; and we ourselves are passing through a silent, gradual, but momentous doubting revolution. What is it that has made the clergymen of all denominations in these later days so temperate in their views, so considerate for the opinions of others? It is Doubt arising from discoveries in science, and from numberless works in which religious topics have been treated with freedom of spirit. Certainly there has been a wonderful change within the last twenty years. When I lived with Dr. Chalmers in London, men spoke of these matters under their breath, but now ladies discuss them freely enough: and I have heard a clergyman of the Church of England say things in the pulpit which in my younger days very few laymen would have dared to say at a dinner- party. Yet in spite of all this progress much religious persecution goes on, and bigotry abounds. The diffusion of Doubt is the only remedy for these evils; and though the hacking and hewing of old beliefs must cause much suffering, it is better that a thousand should suffer rather than that one crime of intolerance should be committed.

I now withdrew from the firm and adopted the pleasant life of the country gentleman, retaining, however, the habits of the scholar. I had determined when I left Limmerleigh never to pass a day without doing a kind action; and also to contribute something every day to the general knowledge of mankind. Having no special talents, I was at first puzzled what to do. However, I thought it might be of use if I translated into popular English some of the great writers of antiquity. This, as you know, has been my daily task for many years, and the works already published attest my industry.

And now a last word about my religion. It has been with me very many years. We are no longer strangers to each other. It has given me peace. It has made me content. It has taught me to value and enjoy life, yet not to dread annihilation.

I believe in God the Incomprehensible, whose nature man can never ascertain. To adore this extraordinary power would be irrational; nor do I allow myself to speculate upon the mystery; for it is wrong to waste the powers of the brain, which might otherwise be usefully employed, in reflecting on problems which cannot be solved.

I continue to gather knowledge, and shall do so to my last hour. I endeavor to be good, and rigidly watch my temper and my thoughts.

I seek the happiness of others. I will own that often in these twenty-five years I have sighed for my old belief, when to me God was semi-human and man was semi-divine; and after death, life began, and happiness never ceased; and my mother, my Margaret, would be joined to me again. And also sometimes my heart has rebelled against the fate of the human race, doomed to work like the coral insects of the sea. But I learnt how to stifle such repinings and regrets; and now I have attained the perfection of unselfishness as regards the disposition of my soul. Last year, when I was given up by the doctors and expected to die every hour, I had no desire whatever to begin a new state of existence; and it even seemed ludicrous to me, the idea of my feeble imperfect mind being transplanted to another world. It was, I thought, just and natural that I should go back to the Earth whence I came.

I have little more to say. I think you will admit, my dear Ellen, that one may cease to believe in a Personal God and in the Immortality of the Soul, and yet not cease to be a good and even a religious man; indeed, I think I have proved something more — namely, that this Religion of Unselfishness, for those who are able to embrace it, is far more ennobling than any religion which holds out the hope of celestial rewards. It may be that precisely on account of its unselfishness and purity it can make but few converts in the present condition of the human mind; and certainly long ages must elapse before it can become the Religion of the World. But I believe that year by year the power of this religion will increase, and that more and more, as time goes on, it will give rest to troubled hearts, as it did to mine at Limmerleigh.

Lastly, there is one thing you ought to understand. I disbelieve in a future life; and this disbelief amounts to a positive conviction. But I may be mistaken, It is impossible to know. The doctrine or theory of a future life is not contrary to reason like that of a Personal Creator. We can show it to be most improbable; but on the other hand we must allow that it is a possible contingency.

Well now, you might say, "Suppose that a good man, converted by your arguments, gave, up the belief in his own immortality, loved others, labored for others, strove to purify his heart, but took no heed for his own soul, and died believing in annihilation and there should be a future life after all — what then? "Why, then he would be perfectly prepared for the life which he did not anticipate. For this is a beautiful quality of our religion. We disbelieve in future rewards, and so eradicate all selfish longings from our hearts; but if, contrary to our expectations, there should be a future life with rewards, none will be able to rank with ourselves. For what life is so highly deserving of reward as that which is spent in doing good without the hope or desire of reward?

www.ingramcontent.com/pod-product-compliance
Lightning Source LLC
Chambersburg PA
CBHW021207020426
42331CB00003B/243